Sunshine in My Soul

DISCOVERING THE MAGIC IN EVERYDAY LIFE

LINDA R. ARCHIBALD

Deseret Book Company
Salt Lake City, Utah

Library of Congress Cataloging-in-Publication Data

Archibald, Linda R., 1942–
    Sunshine in my soul : discovering the magic in everyday life /
Linda R. Archibald.
       p.   cm.
    ISBN 1-57345-555-5
    1. Archibald, Linda R., 1942–   . 2. Mormon women—Biography.
3. Mormon women—Religious life. 4. Mormons—Biography. I. Title.
BX8695.A73A3   1999
289.3'092—dc21
[B]   99-16925
                                              CIP

Printed in the United States of America   54459-6492

10 9   8   7   6   5   4   3   2   1

For Teri

Happiness is the object and design of our existence.

—JOSEPH SMITH

CONTENTS

ACKNOWLEDGMENTS

In addition to my sunshine teachers, Ayrton and Brazil, there have been many who have contributed to the composition and the completion of this book.

Thanks go to:

- Russell Róbe for teaching me the ins and outs of publishing and distribution. Without his infinite patience and fine-tuned professional assistance, this book would still be just a stack of papers on my desk.

- Sheri Dew for willingly listening to me—more than once.

- Jadine Brown, Jeanne Hatch, and Ruth Latimer for compassionate preliminary editing; and Richard Peterson for friendly final editing.

- Bill and Anita Hall for professional and personal support through thick and thin.

- Jean Alder for being the "sounding board" I needed over time.

- Jane Kennedy for listening, reading, giving valuable feedback, and suggesting that a cool glass of lemonade is so refreshing because it is, by nature, full of opposition.

- Carol Jackson, Mary Ann Degn, Janice Warthen, and

Kathleen Russo for kindnesses and philosophies herein recorded.

- Carol Hillam for moments of inspiration, acknowledged and unacknowledged.

- Keith and Lori Dunford, Margot Van Orman, Judy Hill, and Sharon Taylor for reviewing the manuscript.

- Cory and Gayle Bangerter, Pat Holland, and Joanne Tingey for saying the right things at the right times.

- Kirk Jones for incomparable insights.

- Elder Richard G. Scott and the late Sister Scott, and Elder and Sister Neal A. Maxwell for constant encouragement.

- the Gospel Doctrine class of the International Branch in São Paulo for sharing with me so many perceptions on joy.

- and my family (parents, husband, daughter, and more) for giving me the freedom to "learn . . . and get better"; with a very special thanks to Dallas for so many things, but especially for turning on the television set that May morning and for later suggesting I write the story and pushing me over the hurdles.

All of you have made my life brighter and more beautiful!

INTRODUCTION

Searching for Sunshine

You can make the pathway bright,
Fill the soul with heaven's light,
If there's sunshine in your heart;
Turning darkness into day,
As the shadows fly away,
If there's sunshine in your heart today.
("You Can Make the Pathway Bright,"
Hymns, no. 228)

So many times I had sung those words and enjoyed the lilting pace of the song, like children skipping through a summer meadow; but in all those melodious moments I never realized that the words were an invitation to a lifestyle. I never knew, I really never knew, that the sunshine that makes the pathway bright comes from inside, from the heart. I assumed that it occasionally beamed in from somewhere "out there," providing momentary warmth and peace.

I have many favorite songs in the hymn book: "Praise to the Man," "How Great Thou Art," "There Is a Green Hill Far Away," "Lord, I Would Follow Thee," and "Hark, All Ye Nations!" just to name a few (*Hymns*, nos. 27, 86, 194, 220,

264). The difference between those songs and "You Can Make the Pathway Bright" is that the others have become favorites as my testimony of the gospel has deepened, while "Pathway" has been a favorite for as long as I can remember.

Because of the length of time that the melody about sunshine has been skipping through my mind and my life, it is unbelievable that I never recognized the power in its message. I didn't realize that where sunshine is concerned, I have an individual responsibility to create that resplendent joy.

I have also "tripped over" sunshine principles in the scriptures, but with them, too, I've rushed on without grasping their significance.

"Adam fell that men might be; and men are, that they might have joy" (2 Nephi 2:25).

"Let us be glad and rejoice" (Revelation 19:7).

"A merry heart doeth good like a medicine" (Proverbs 17:22).

Because I could neither define nor internalize these happy thoughts, I hadn't even considered trying to teach them to others.

Although my temporal life was comfortable and my testimony was firm, sunshine remained a rare commodity as "joy" and I played hide-and-seek. On occasion I would find the sparkle, and it would stream in and light up my life, but soon it would dissipate like elusive sunbeams. I relegated the hope of obtaining any kind of long-lasting, real, honest-to-goodness joy to the future, for I didn't see much of it being available in mortality. Life, I assumed, was very serious business, a rather turbulent endeavor requiring persistent concentration. Of course I knew people who continually danced past me and around me, but I viewed them as slightly eccentric.

Many who know me may be surprised at this confession of personal weariness, but those who know me best will concur that I once walked daily with a discontent I had learned to publicly suppress. I was a perfectionist with a long list of unrealistic and, therefore, unmet expectations. Some of life's greatest challenges are found in our efforts to deal with the invisible weaknesses and limitations hidden inside our minds and hearts.

Then one "magic" day in Brazil, I learned the truth in an illuminating experience of magnificent proportions. Such eye-openers are always something of a miracle, and my change of heart certainly was. So many enchanting ingredients were there that day: gratitude, faith, and love; emotion, spontaneity and, yes, even sunshine. But I would still have missed the message if the Spirit had not focused my attention, guided my thoughts, and given me personalized instruction. The Lord always knows exactly how to "turn the night to day" (*Hymns*, no. 228) in each of us, individually, if we will just request assistance and then stop, look, and listen.

What took place was unusual, untraditional, unexpected, and, in a way, unbelievable. Yet the event was completely authentic—totally genuine. All the lessons didn't become clear to me immediately, but on that day I began to understand; and over several months, like fireworks going off in a chain reaction, what I observed and felt lit up my life with sunshine and taught me the meaning of joy.

What happened on that magical day convinced me that, even with the gospel in my life, I had been wilting in the shadows, allowing joy to slip through my fingers.

At first glance, Brazil may seem to be just a nation of ordinary people, and their hero, Ayrton Senna, a champion auto-racing driver, may appear to be just an ordinary athlete. I submit, however, that neither the Brazilian people nor Ayrton Senna are at all ordinary. Of course, one could certainly argue that I am significantly biased in this claim, but I believe their magic stands as its own historical witness of their uncommon light. In a few short hours they "sent a shining ray" that "turned the night to day" and confirmed that joy is, most of all, a song of the heart.

In truth, when that day began I did not know the people well even though I had lived among them for years, and their hero I knew not at all; but this lack of knowledge was powerless to prevent their impact on my life. As joy rose victorious, I heard the music. Afterward, I learned even more from them and from him. I learned a complete composition, and sunshine came to stay.

Imagine my surprise when I discovered all of us should be dancing sprightly along the path during our earthly sojourn. The pioneers did it nightly on their trek West. Singing with vigor is also highly recommended: "For my soul delighteth in the song of the heart; yea, the song of the righteous is a prayer unto me . . ." (D&C 25:12).

My solemn perspective of persistently plodding along

was a delusion. Honorable "eccentrics" wring all the good out of life; and those on the strait and narrow path not only know the gospel is true, they also know how to *live* the gospel. If I were going to join them, I had to begin to dance, to sing, to trade melancholy for merriment, gloom for gladness, sadness for sunshine. I had to follow the counsel of President Gordon B. Hinckley: " . . . in all of living have much of fun and laughter. Life is to be enjoyed, not just endured" (*Ensign*, May 1996, 94).

Before that magic day, I didn't know how to change. I didn't know I was supposed to change. Perhaps I didn't even want to change. Pessimism can be habit-forming, and the doldrums of self-pity can provide artificial protection from life's unexplored seas, allowing us to row aimlessly in circles around our comfort zones. As I made an about-face on that day, with course corrections executed intermittently during the months which followed, I made a commitment to accept the challenge which accompanies joy: to do more, to be more, to believe more. Joy—sunshine in your heart—carries a responsibility to stretch.

My experience that day was personal, therefore my perceptions and opinions are also personal and are my responsibility alone. I suppose the events which acted as catalyst could be viewed in as many different ways as there were people watching, and there were millions. Time and distance now separate me from the day and the place. Even so, the magic still follows me, reminding me that the greatest miracle of all is when hearts are changed. Mere words are sometimes inadequate to describe such a metamorphosis;

nevertheless, in the following pages I have attempted to explain how my cocoon fell away and how I learned to soar in the sunshine.

Initially the glow, the radiance, burst into my life like the day dawn breaking. I was spellbound by the truth. In spite of this, learning to sing the "sunshine serenade" was no quick and easy process. I practiced and practiced and practiced the principles. In doing so, I became aware that when we have difficulty holding onto joy we may not know how to trade gloom for gladness, melancholy for merriment, sadness for sunshine. For most of us, exchanging pessimism for optimism requires effort. Just as faith and testimony must be carefully tended in order to grow, gospel joy must be nurtured in order to endure.

In due time, I realized that those much-sought-after sunbeams are not elusive after all. They are always there, like a vast congregation of fireflies frolicking in a meadow. We can end the game of hide-and-seek by simply facing in their direction, allowing them to light up our lives inside and out. They only seem to evaporate when we turn away.

Joy is initially a personal choice, a desire and a decision to put in sufficient effort to face the light regardless of external circumstances. Afterward, as with other gospel qualities, our joy can be increased, becoming more brilliant and secure each day as we, through the help of the Spirit, learn to live this important principle.

Without question there are those beyond the scope of our mortal vision—Satan and his legions—who have no sunshine in their hearts and who will do everything they can to pull us into their discouraging circle of unhappy campers. We have the power to dispel their influence, the seeds of pessimism and despair, if we but begin the quest for sunshine.

> If there's sunshine in your heart,
> You can send a shining ray
> That will turn the night to day;
> And your cares will all depart,
> If there's sunshine in your heart today.
> (*Hymns*, no. 228)

The music of that Brazilian day, *my* magic day, still sings to me in perfect harmony; and I know that anyone who is willing to practice the principles can learn the song. I first heard that song clearly on a day in May when a remarkable symphony of light made life brighter and more beautiful for everyone watching, even through the tears.

FROM SHADOWS TO SUNSHINE

THE MAGIC OF
ONE BRAZILIAN DAY

I did not see the love affair blossom and bloom between Brazilians and their hero. I was not watching on the day the hero died. But I did witness his final homecoming and the events of the next day-and-a-half, which were crowned with magic. The magic took me down the straightaway of life at dazzling speed—out of the shadows, into the sunshine.

In the magic—the power of faith, hope, gratitude, and love—I learned the truth:

> Weeping may endure for a night, but joy cometh in the morning (Psalm 30:5).

PRELUDE : THE LOVE AFFAIR

Ayrton Senna of Brazil, three-time world champion of prestigious Formula 1 automobile racing, was considered by

1

many to be the fastest and best race driver in the world. In Brazil, where "racing-fever" is almost as much a passion as the national epidemic "soccer-fever," Senna's name was always in the headlines; but his array of trophies, his international celebrity status, and his mounting fortune, by themselves, cannot explain the national adoration.

Although he spent most of every year propelling nimble Formula 1 race cars around renowned Grand Prix racing circuits throughout the world, his heart never really left home. Brazil's green, yellow, and blue were his personal colors; and in his innate patriotism, Brazil had both a natural advocate and an articulate spokesman. Then, by chance, on a July day in 1986 he became a hero, a legend, and the catalyst for a dream.

That year had been a discouraging one for Brazil, with crime, rampant inflation, and political disappointment all on the rise. However, since it was a World Cup soccer year, those challenges were set aside.

Soccer is the lifeblood of Brazil.

Once every four years for an entire month, the nations of the earth convene for the worldwide World Cup soccer tournament, and Brazilian enthusiasm vibrates with great expectations for their famous, and often favored, all-star team. In any given World Cup year, Brazilians believe they deserve to take the trophy home, and 1986 was no exception. They could almost taste the sweetness of ultimate victory—even though their team had experienced some dry years, not having won the championship since 1970, during the glory days of soccer super star, Pelé.

Brazilians are blessed with a natural buoyancy and have often been described as the most optimistic people in the world; but, even for such people, occasionally the light goes out.

In an early round of World Cup competition, France eliminated mighty Brazil from the tournament. In that crushing defeat, Brazil's last hope of salvaging dwindling self-respect vanished, and national pride crumbled. That long World Cup dry spell had just gone on too long, and the accumulated social problems were too much. The events left the nation in shock. That July day, wherever a Brazilian was found, there was also found despair and a broken heart.

The next day, at a Formula 1 race in the United States, a young, promising Brazilian driver named Ayrton Senna surveyed the crowd, searching unsuccessfully for the sight of even one Brazilian flag.

Formula 1 racing has a distinctive, multinational atmosphere, drawing drivers from many different countries and with Grand Prix tracks located all over Europe and on almost every other continent. Even though the competition is between automobile companies and builders, not between nations, fans always bring national flags to the races as incentive and recognition for their favorite drivers or for drivers from their home countries—and the gala Brazilian cheering section invariably makes its presence known.

On this particular day, however, the suffering, despondent Brazilian contingent was hiding its green, yellow, and blue flags. Senna sensed that a similar dark cloud of failure and unfulfilled dreams hung heavily over his Brazil, half a world away.

He, too, felt disappointment; but his love for his homeland and his faith in its people could not be suppressed.

In a sparkling race performance that day, Senna rocketed into the lead and held it all the way to the winning checkered flag—creating more than a little irony by whizzing across the finish line just ahead of two cars piloted by drivers from France.

Looking to the stands and finally seeing a few Brazilian flags fluttering, he spontaneously pulled to the side of the track before beginning his victory lap. He motioned to a nearby Brazilian spectator to bring him a flag. Then holding that banner high, he proudly rounded the track, lifting the spirits of his countrymen and taking their hearts with him as he climbed to the winner's podium. He compelled Brazilian audiences everywhere to look up and, when they did, they saw Senna and their flag triumphant. His faith undaunted and his allegiance secure, he invited others to follow his lead.

In that instant, his love for Brazil was set free, and he became his nation's beacon, and its people became his people.

Watching, in person or via TV, Brazilians lit a "torch" from Senna's fire and then kindled additional joy by telling others of his magic.

During the week, the story was retold in World Cup crowds.

The media sent the images of Brazil's "hope restored" around the world.

And Brazilians once again unfurled their green, yellow, and blue flags.

Almost overnight, the young and promising racing driver became universally known as "Ayrton Senna of Brazil." The power of his light and love had vanquished clouds of gloom and mended broken hearts. Feeding off his exuberance, his people reclaimed the joy they had lost.

After that, as he rewrote racing record books and often snatched success from the jaws of imminent defeat, it became a tradition for him to display the green, yellow, and blue flag during every victory lap. In these exhilarating moments, a bouncy, toe-tapping tune—his original victory theme—announced to the world that the Brazilian flag was once again flying high. By these simple deeds, he effectively transmitted his unique message of faith and encouragement across the miles and gave his people a vision of personal and national victory.

In response, Brazil developed an epidemic of "Senna-fever," which infected all of society, without regard for age, gender, or social status. On the strength of his inspiration and example, every dream seemed possible.

Over the next few years, in his singular way, he honored them by his successes, and the Brazilian people basked in the events of his life and his love. They reveled in his sincerity and sensitivity; his kindness and compassion; his enthusiasm for life; his firm emphasis on God, family, and country. Always unpretentious, he tried to decline hero status, but to no avail. He was their knight in shining armor, for he generated self-esteem and confidence and sent it racing home to them.

Throughout the world, wherever Formula 1 racing is ardently followed, Ayrton Senna's genuine blend of discipline, charm, and authenticity was idolized, even revered. Men admired him. Women loved him. Children worshipped him.

And in his Brazil, where 150 million people always claim an extra portion of summer warmth and light, every day was brighter and more beautiful because he was their sunshine.

NIGHTFALL

That first day of May 1994 dawned beautifully, full of hope and promise. In Italy, at the San Marino Grand Prix, Senna was leading the pack of spirited Formula 1 racing machines. Suddenly—during the 7th lap, at the high-speed Tamburello curve—a mechanical failure caused his blue car to veer off the track and propelled him directly toward an unprotected concrete wall. In a fraction of a second, Senna shifted down two gears and applied maximum braking effort, but nothing could change the location of the wall. A streak of blue splattered against it. The fragile car exploded in a shower of tires and metal parts, spinning up and out in every direction.

When the chaos settled and the remains of his car slid to a stop, the anxious millions watching worldwide expected him to step safely from the driver's seat as he had so often done before. When he didn't, they begged him to stand up, even commanded him. But there was no response.

In those first few minutes after the crash, no one knew that a whirling piece of debris had exploded with lethal intensity through the front of his yellow helmet. The fans held their breath while the emergency medical team lifted his body from the wreckage.

Because of Senna's indomitable will, he had always seemed invincible; but the blood-soaked linen left on the Italian race track said otherwise.

An incredulous Brazilian nation looked on in total disbelief, unprepared to accept that his hand would never again hold their flag, that his great heart had ceased beating. When his death was officially announced, flags nationwide fell to half-mast. Black banners and streamers were solemnly affixed to buildings and vehicles. An oppressive hush settled over the country. A flood of tears extinguished all light.

Darkness descended in a total eclipse of their sun.

Homecoming

As the plane bearing his body from Europe touched down in the pre-dawn hours of May fourth, the crowd at the international airport in São Paulo, Brazil, huddled closer together as if by touching each other they could summon needed strength. Many of them had waited there throughout the night.

They looked on, heartbroken, as the polished, red wooden casket was removed from the plane and ceremoniously carried by military pallbearers to a platform on the back of a waiting fire truck. There a green, yellow, and blue Brazilian flag was reverently draped over the coffin. Four guards took their places, two on each side of the casket, and the vehicle began to slowly move forward.

Morning was now breaking, and a subdued multitude lined the roads leading out of the airport. The fire truck inched through the masses, occasionally stopping, persuading them to move aside. And they did. They had come out of respect and love. There was no desire to interfere.

Hundreds of thousands, from all segments of society, lined the route from the airport to downtown São Paulo, and tears flowed as the truck came into view and they saw the truth for themselves.

They had lost their inspiration, their hero.

From the airport, the cortege moved mournfully through the city to the Legislative Assembly Hall where Senna's closed casket was to lie in state for twenty-four continuous hours. During that short time, even throughout the night, a quarter of a million disconsolate men, women, and children steadily passed by, in single file, with never a break in the line.

Outside on the grounds, wreaths and flower bouquets by the hundreds accumulated. Television transported the images to every corner of the country. Minutes evolved into hours, yet time seemed to stand still.

Daylight dimmed. The sun set. The shroud tightened around Brazil.

And a melancholy rendition of a once bouncy victory tune drifted somberly over the land, a haunting requiem to the end of a dream.

But then suddenly, in the dark: a pulse, a spark, a sliver of light! Magic stirred spontaneously in the hearts of the people. Although they felt destitute, a kaleidoscope of memories reminded Brazilians that they were *his* people and black was not *his* color. They had a debt to pay and a legacy to fulfill. Ever so thankful that they had been his students for a brief season, one by one they vowed to acknowledge the love he had given and honor him as he had honored them. Because he taught them to believe, they would force the sun to shine once more.

And so it came to pass that glittering rays of gratitude shattered the darkness. The next day dawned radiant, and a jubilant people wrapped their tribute in green, yellow, and blue.

So many people. So many flags. So many cheers.

Not many months before, Senna had traveled the streets of São Paulo as the world champion of speed. On that day, he was honored with passionate applause and the rhythmic chant that followed him everywhere: "Olé! Olé! Olé! Olá! Senna! Senna!"

Now he would traverse the avenues of his hometown one final time, praised in reverent jubilation as a champion of life.

More than a million people poured into the streets,

filling sidewalks, overpasses, balconies, and rooftops to over-flowing along the route from the Assembly Hall to the cemetery. They had an earnest message to deliver and, in faith, they believed that somehow he would see, somehow he would hear.

Patiently, tearfully, anxiously they waited.

At the Assembly Hall, military pallbearers again gently lifted the red wooden casket to their shoulders. Slowly they carried him down a red carpet, between mounds of floral tributes, to a final reunion with his people. Cascades of rose petals fluttered down upon him; the flag he loved once again embraced him. The fire truck received its precious cargo, and regal mounted cavalry formed an honor guard as the journey began.

A dozen flag bearers on both sides of the main tree-lined boulevard bid him welcome. Twirling multicolored banners, they presented the traditional Formula 1 salute to the vic-tor. Ayrton Senna had won his last race. More than that, he had won their hearts.

The crowd immediately responded to the advancing procession, unfurling a sea of Brazilian flags and drenching the air with the sound of triumphant yet tender applause. Mile after mile, in his last victory lap, those thousands upon thousands awarded him a united, unanimous standing ova-tion. Like a wave, the acclaim carried him on and on across the city.

Tears fell, even though they cheered: "Olé! Olé! Olé! Olá! Senna! Senna!"

In the distance, cannons fired in tribute. In the streets,

confetti danced in the sunlight and floated down to rest around him.

And everywhere on display were countless banners and posters, both professional and homemade, which passionately proclaimed the sunshine in each heart:

> "Ayrton Senna, forever!"
> "Thanks, Ayrton, for the joy!"
> "Life is eternal. We'll see you soon."
> "It was worth it, Senna."
> "Thank you! Thank you! Thank you!"

The fervor of their resounding praise never faltered, never dimmed—until the emotional journey ended on a carpet of green grass at the cemetery. A hush returned to the land as brief graveside services conducted for family and friends were officially recorded by telephoto lens and beamed by TV across the nation.

At the conclusion of the ceremony, the inspiration of his music once more flowed out across the airwaves. This time the melody was a concert of triumph in tragedy: a declaration of anguished hearts, a commitment to a living dream. The message flooded Brazil with nostalgia, hope, and treasured memories.

As the power of the symphony soared, military planes lifted the boundless adoration heavenward. They flew high above the cemetery and, with their vapor trails, drew his trademark letter S and a majestic valentine heart in the clear blue sky.

At that moment, all Brazil stopped in silent tribute and the collective soul of the country, torn between pain and appreciation, was compelled to look up—into the sunshine.

"Farewell, Senna," it whispered as the magic of the day took flight.

His students had learned their lessons well, and their love had been set free.

EPILOGUE

Two months later, after twenty-four dry years, the Brazilian soccer team once again claimed the World Cup crown.

Throughout the weeks of the tournament, team members prayed together, held hands in unity, overcame personal ego, and finally emerged victorious from the triple overtime of the championship game. All their effort and solidarity had but one special purpose: to give Senna's people a long-awaited, rejuvenating donation of sunshine.

Exhausted, but elated at having achieved their hearts' desires, the Brazilian all-star team raised the green, yellow, and blue flag high as they dedicated the victory to Senna's memory.

Although time passes and months turn into years, Senna's people continually carry flags and flowers to the cemetery. There they bridge time and space, remembering the gifts he gave from his heart. And they reflect on the power of sunshine.

The warmth of their farewell on that magic day in May

served to lighten their pain, ease their sorrow. Still they feel a void, an ache without him, a yearning for his presence, which ensures that their gratitude for his faith and friendship will always endure. Their words, recorded on billboards in São Paulo a few days after the funeral, have become reality:

"Thank you, Ayrton Senna!
You will live forever in our hearts!"

They loved him then, they always will, because he first loved them—unconditionally.

A HEART IN
THE SKY

I have witnessed several remarkable epic funerals during my lifetime. Of them all, only Senna's initiated an emotional about-face and turned the night to day. I had never seen such a dramatic demonstration of personal power.

The events were unusual and untraditional; yet they were also so right, so memorable, so magical in the way they made a perfect blend of suffering and sunshine—both elements equally intense, equally genuine, completely intertwined.

As that vapor-trail-heart floated silently in the sky over the green cemetery not far from where I lived, I experienced a similar contrast of pain and light, which swirled around me, creating an emotion, a euphoria that made me feel so very much alive. My tears fell for Brazil and its people, for the loss of their hero and for their heroic tribute. At the same time, I knew some of those tears were wrung from opposition deep within my soul. They were squeezed from the pain of over a decade of lost opportunities yet released in light because, for me, morning had broken. I had seen and heard a most amazing joyousness and, although my personal transformation was only beginning, I had experienced a mighty change of heart.

I was suddenly in love with a place and a people I had been crosswise with for years.

As a result of my husband's work in international business, São Paulo had been my home for more than eleven years. Prior to living in Brazil, we had resided in several states of the United States and in various foreign countries—from Japan to the Philippines, South Africa to Venezuela, Spain to Mexico. These moves always meant adapting to new cultural patterns, new customs, new procedures, and, sometimes, new languages. For me, the adjustments had never been easy. Upon arriving in Brazil, however, I was certain that this transfer would go more smoothly than the others. After all, I had a lot of experience to draw on.

But within a short time, I ran into unexpected, difficult challenges. My ability to speak Spanish did not guarantee rapid assimilation of Brazil's Portuguese. Living in other large cities did not prepare me for São Paulo's concrete jungle of 20 million people. And Brazilians nationwide generally demonstrated more sunshine and spontaneity than I could adjust to in my world of well-ordered solemnity. Even on good days, I was careful and troubled. Even in trying times, Brazilians are fun-loving and happy. In Brazil, a long wait in a long line often turns into a jovial social gathering, and a traffic jam can erupt into a samba party. Life can be tough in Brazil, but living is seldom seen as serious business.

As a result of the friction I felt from my inability to

blend in, I quickly constructed a "wall"—a very high, very strong, albeit invisible "wall"—built of critical feelings, harsh judgments, and resentment. Since Brazil was different than I wanted and expected, I separated myself from it as much as possible. I murmured about the language, the place, and the people—and retreated into my narrow comfort zone.

In hindsight, I can see that quite often, during many special moments, a few bricks were knocked away from my fortress of discontent, but I always conscientiously put them right back again. There were even times and seasons when I encountered such beauty that the entire wall should have fallen; but I, single-handedly, held it in place through stubborn pessimism because I had neither ears to hear nor eyes to see. Cynicism obscures truth, unrighteous judgment negates understanding, and resentment buries love.

Even though I managed to become adequately fluent in Portuguese, carried on necessary and amiable associations with the people, and learned to traverse the city, I remained separate and apart, always retreating to my own side of the barricade I had erected.

Because of my isolation from Brazil and because I never followed Formula 1 racing, I knew nothing about Ayrton Senna when I first heard brief mention of his death. I was unaware of his universal appeal and had no understanding of the impact his death would have on his homeland.

More to the point, I wasn't even interested.

I spent the next couple of days behind the wall in my own little world, far removed from the heart-wrenching grief that was being felt. I did not know the people were suffering, waiting for their hero to come home one final time.

Because I was totally oblivious to the approaching events, I would never have thought to turn on the television that May fourth morning. Fortunately for me, my husband tuned in and called my attention to the images being beamed into my living room: a flag-draped casket on a fire truck moving slowly through the crowds lining the roads at the airport.

As I glanced at the TV screen, I vaguely remembered hearing something about a Brazilian racing champion (what was his name?) who had died; but for me, ignoring Brazil was a way of life, and I had no desire to change.

Intending to leave the room to continue my chores, I was surprised to find myself riveted in place. So I stood there, without knowing why, mechanically watching the mourning and the tears.

Finally I sat down to follow the video rerun of the plane returning from Europe and landing at the airport in those early morning hours: the ceremony, the sadness, the adoration of a hero.

Eventually I became a participant in their drama. I went in search of a box of tissues and surrendered to my tears—for the people, for him, and for the loss and the tragedy.

As I watched the events, I found I was fascinated by the replays of scenes from his life: his unassuming smile, the wave of his hand to the crowd, his obvious confidence combined with an air of shyness; fast machines, checkered flags,

Brazilian flags—and over and over again, the flash of his blue car as it shattered against a concrete wall somewhere in Italy.

Watching him in those images from the past, I began to sense his sincerity. Though I still knew almost nothing about him, I began to understand why they grieved and how much they would miss him. I wondered why someone who spread so much joy in life had to leave it so early.

I followed the scenes to the Assembly Hall where the atmosphere was heavy with grief and with love. The soldiers carried him so tenderly. His family and close friends were so understanding of everyone's need to have a second or two to say good-bye; and, indeed, everyone appeared to be his friend, maybe even a member of his family—the family of Brazil.

Hypnotized by the drama, all that day I absorbed every detail, reluctant to move beyond the reach of the television. Late into the night, sleep finally overcame me; yet I relived the day's happenings over and over in my dreams.

The next morning I was up early, anticipating their final tribute. As I watched the TV coverage of the procession, feeling the fusion of heartache and appreciation, I soaked tissue after tissue with tears.

"His people" were inspiring. I wanted to cheer for them—and for him.

Because I was bound to the events so tightly, I wasn't conscious of the change in me until the planes decorated the sky with that wispy heart. At that moment, the intense connection began to ebb and I knew that something within me had become very different. The realization was small and subtle at first, but it mounted in crescendo until I was filled with astonishment.

My wall had fallen!

Throughout that morning, the once impenetrable fortress had been bombarded by so much gratitude, faith, and love that, finally, weakened beyond repair, it crumbled and light streamed in. Through the years I had refused to join them, but now my tears had mingled with theirs, and the union had set me free.

With no self-imposed obstruction to limit my view, I clearly saw the beauty that was and is uniquely Brazilian, and found myself in love with the language, the place, and the people. Bathed in the love, my sharp but fleeting pain over lost opportunities was healed, and I rejoiced in the light—the joy—of the morning. With that joy I wanted to soar heavenward, capture that inspirational heart in the sky and take it home to hang, like a wreath, on my front door. I wanted that day in May to live with me forever.

The wall in Brazil was not the first I had built, neither was it the first that had fallen. It was, however, the largest, and the fall of it was great. Sufficiently humbled, I vowed never to build another like it, and I knew I would keep the promise. Brazil's magic had permanently dismantled my defenses and initiated the downfall of pessimism. I, too, had been compelled to look up—into the sunshine.

With this new perspective, this new light, came the recognition of other walls in my life, other negative attitudes (most of which had no connection to foreign countries) that had affected my relationships and my outlook. So I began a search-and-destroy mission to eliminate those barriers, some large and some small, which I had built here and there. Some fell easily. Others needed to be weakened by something akin to dynamite and, after detonation, still required continual chipping away over time; but I was more than willing to keep all necessary tools handy. I finally understood that to accept, forgive, and see the good in everything is the pathway to loving life. In spite of all the tribulations of mortality, we live in a wonderful world. Without walls, the sun shines in.

Once I felt the freedom achieved by eliminating walls, I wondered why so many of us build those barriers. We are all children of our Father in Heaven. We lived together in the royal courts on high, and I'm sure there were none of those walls there. We were, we are, "sons and daughters, children of a King" ("Called to Serve," *Hymns*, no. 249). We are royalty!

True, with all our individual mortal weaknesses, we don't always look or act like princes and princesses. That is one of the consequences of earth life. But the existence of personal limitations does not change the facts. When we accentuate the positive and eliminate the negative, suddenly the worth of every soul is great (see D&C 18:10).

No, we're not perfect—not one of us. We all make mistakes. We even make fools of ourselves occasionally. We're all in this mortal boat together, so why should we judge others? In fact, the Lord is quite clear about people who judge.

When Moroni sensed that the Gentiles might make fun of his writing and mock him and his people, he was told that it would be the fools who would mock (see Ether 12:26).

Ah! So the person who is trying, no matter the outcome, is not the fool after all. The fool is the one with the pointing finger!

People who point fingers are simultaneously building walls.

I was reading in the book of Alma, chapter 10, when I learned why those walls are so effective at holding light at bay. In verse six, Alma's missionary companion, Amulek, explains the reasons for his long-term rejection of gospel principles: "Nevertheless, *I did harden my heart,* for I was called many times and I would not hear; therefore I knew concerning these things, yet I would not know; therefore I went on rebelling against God, in the wickedness of my heart" (emphasis added).

As I internalized the words, I reluctantly sensed a relationship between Amulek's experience of being called many times and my experience with the wall I had mortared back together so often. Then, feeling the weight of the implications, I attempted to deny the parallels.

"Whoa and wait a minute! Hardened my heart? HARD-ENED MY HEART? What do you mean, 'HARDENED MY HEART?' I didn't harden my heart! I just built a wall—a distant, impersonal barricade! Hard hearts are for Laman and Lemuel and Sodom and Gomorrah and those who work iniquity. Not me! I hadn't hardened my heart!"

But as I read the verse again and then again, I came to

see that I was building a wall between me and Alma 10:6. So I took a deep breath, closed my eyes, and leveled it, eliminating the contention. Who was I, after all, to argue with Amulek? A rose by any other name is still a rose, and a hard heart by any other name is still a hard heart. Anytime we separate ourselves from God, His children, or the works of His hands, we have hardened our hearts. Hard hearts are barriers we build, manifest in murmuring, which bind us and keep us from recognizing beauty and truth though we may be called over and over again. Only with time does the darkness created by those walls translate to evil and open rebellion for those who become "past feeling" (1 Nephi 17:45).

When we allow our hearts to solidify within us, there can be no "pathway bright." Sunshine cannot penetrate hearts of stone.

On that magic day in Brazil, there was virtually no crime in São Paulo. Everyone was too busy mourning together and comforting each other to cause trouble. Every Brazilian in every location claimed a personal portion of the message sent via that special valentine in the sky: "Farewell, Senna—with all our love." There was unity—no walls, no hard hearts, anywhere. For a few hours, just as in the golden era described in the Book of Mormon, "there was no contention in the land . . . nor any manner of -ites; but they were in one" (4 Nephi 1:15–17).

In spite of the heartache, there was joy that day in Brazil—the joy of gospel principles in action. Brazilians had pushed the "override buttons" in their minds and hearts and allowed faith, hope, gratitude, and love to supersede the pain. Grief was overlaid with sunshine, and the sunshine was contagious.

I, for one, would never be the same.

MAKING
LEMONADE

Late in the afternoon of that day in May, I traveled part of the route the cortege took through the streets of São Paulo. Flags on poles fluttered at half-mast while the breeze ruffled a host of others draped from window sills in apartment and office buildings. Countless banners of gratitude still proclaimed their sincere message. Confetti speckled the streets. Best of all, a marvelous magic, quiet but electric, tarried in the air. The outpouring of love had lingered long after the crowds had left and I knew that, for me, the magic would always be there.

The banners remained in place for weeks, attached to buildings and trees and telephone poles. No one wanted to take them down and break the spell. Throughout the country, green and yellow billboards joined those banners in São Paulo to express the emotions of a nation. "Farewell Champion" proclaimed the tribute in Brasilia, while far to the north in Recife the message included faith and a silver lining: "Thanks, Senna. We miss you, but there is joy in heaven!"

Senna and his people, like other "eccentrics," knew how

to wring all the good out of life. They really understood the meaning of the directive: "When life gives you lemons, make lemonade!" Never again would that time-worn phrase seem mundane or absurd to me. In spite of the "lemons" life had rained on them, overnight Senna's people gathered up all the "sugar" they could find and poured it along the streets of São Paulo, creating an incredible "lemonade" as the cortege passed by.

Without doubt that tribute was the grandest, most awesome display of turning lemons into lemonade that I had ever seen; and I concluded that if it were possible for an entire nation to make lemonade from such lemons, then lemonade was available to anyone, anytime, anywhere. One only needed the right recipe, one that reads something like this:

1. Think of good "stuff" and rejoice in it.
2. Don't hold back genuine, positive emotions.
3. Add a dash of spontaneity.
4. Focus on the present moment and make memories by seasoning with hope, gratitude, and love.

Remember, lemonade is a sunshine color. Lemonade is sunshine.

> If there's sunshine in your heart,
> You can send a shining ray
> That will turn the night to day;
> And your cares will all depart,

MAKING LEMONADE

If there's sunshine in your heart today.
(*Hymns*, no. 228)

If . . . If . . . If . . . What an interesting, life-changing word. A personal choice word. We can either look for the silver lining or through a glass darkly. We can accentuate the positive or the negative. We can complain about the lemons life rains down on us or we can take them home and make lemonade.

Geraldine Bangerter, wife of Elder W. Grant Bangerter, tells of a time on a long-term overseas assignment when life seemed all uphill—full of more discomfort, inconvenience, stress, and challenge than anyone could effectively deal with. Her husband entered the scene at the moment her rubber band of patience broke. Her tears began to fall in rivers as she itemized the insurmountable mountain of intolerable situations she was facing. He responded with a smile and a chuckle.

"Look," he proposed in words something like this, "someday we'll laugh about all of this, so why wait? Let's enjoy it now!" With that incentive she tranquilized her discontent, wiped away the tears, and they began to giggle together (see "Enjoy It!" *Ensign*, June 1991, 45).

When I first read that experience, I knew so little about sunshine that I thought the Bangerters were at least eccentric, maybe even a bit crazy. Analyzing the story again after learning the true genesis of sunshine, I realized they had both simply, courageously, exercised their agency and chosen light, joy, and a merry heart.

Sister Bangerter's crisis and change of heart also occurred in that sunshine place, Brazil. Some years later, Ayrton Senna would tell his people: "When you're not happy, you need to be strong to change." That formula requires having "true grit," but, as his people demonstrated one beautiful day in May, when implemented irrevocably, it is foolproof.

We can turn "darkness into day, as the shadows fly away" or we can leave the shadows there. How we view things is all up to us. The "Pathway Bright" song emphasizes our personal power by reminding us, at least five times, "You *can* . . ."

In the well-known children's story titled *The Little Engine That Could*, we read about a tiny train engine, which, in spite of its small size, agrees to pull a load of toys to children who live over the mountain. Motivated by a sense of mission, the engine begins the steep climb, exerting all the energy it can muster, all the while providing verbal self-motivation: "I think I can. I think I can. I think I can."

The monologue continues as the engine struggles up and up against the odds. Then, amazingly, the little train reaches the crest of the hill, and, both exhausted and exhilarated by its victory, rolls down the other side chanting cheerfully, "I thought I could. I thought I could. I thought I could" (Watty Piper, Platt and Monk Pub., N.Y., 1969).

Most people seem to be searching for an easier way—for some means of making the hills less steep or a way to avoid all cares and troubles. The truth about life's challenges is that they respond to being acted upon. They level out when we confront them, solve them, and/or banish them through mental or physical personal power.

The little engine could have spent all day at the bottom of the hill measuring the height of the mountain and worrying about the degree of difficulty. Instead, he simply took action.

In a time full of cares and troubles, Nephi put his foot down: "I will go and do . . ." and the problem was eventually solved (see 1 Nephi 3:7).

Paul reflected, "I have fought a good fight, I have finished my course, I have kept the faith" (2 Timothy 4:7). No sign of endless hand-wringing and immobilization there.

All of us have the power to push ourselves beyond our normal limits. We can transcend life's unbidden troubles and achieve our goals. The seemingly unreachable stars really aren't inaccessible.

We *can!* If we just invite a little sunshine into our hearts.

At the General Young Women Meeting held in the Salt Lake Tabernacle in March 1996, two young women spoke about the sunshine they had found as a result of listening to President Gordon B. Hinckley's teachings on optimism and personal power.

A young woman, Anne Prescott, recounted that her father had passed away shortly before Christmas, casting a pall over the approaching holidays. Then President Hinckley made a surprise visit to her stake conference.

"He bore his testimony and expressed his love. He said: 'Do you feel gloomy? Lift your eyes. Stand on your feet. Sing songs of Christmas. Be positive.' These few words meant so much to me. I knew if I did my best at this hard time in my life, things would work out. What President Hinckley said did not take away my pain, but it helped me understand that I needed to be happy and help my mom and family be happy" (*Ensign*, May 1996, 89).

Another young woman, Anne Marie Rose, explained the discouragement and resentment that invaded her life after a disappointing experience in school sports. She heard President Hinckley's address in general conference. "[He] offered the counsel I needed to put things into perspective. By having an 'overpowering spirit of optimism' and enthusiasm (*Ensign*, Nov. 1995, 72), I could *decide* to let go of my volleyball experience. I could *decide* to be positive and optimistic about the many good things in my life. . . .

"I am grateful for a living prophet who taught me to let go of feeling sorry for myself" (*Ensign*, May 1996, 87).

Yes, we can all *decide!* We can *choose* to sing the "sunshine serenade!"

Although mortality has its moments when there seem to be no answers or relief from trials and troubles, the burdens need not press us into petrified rock. Even if the cares remain, we can still clean the house, weed the garden, walk a mile, read the scriptures, find some happy thoughts, sing a song, maybe even lift someone else's burden to get our minds off our own.

Where lemonade and sunshine are concerned, a little mind control—determination and tenacity—goes a long way.

All this dynamic personal power results from an ability to see beyond the trial and the challenge, to conquer hopelessness with vision and replace despair with hope.

Hope is the primary ingredient in lemonade. Hope enables us to look on the bright side, see the sunny side, make the best of it, take heart, be of good cheer, think of good things and rejoice, and push the "override button" in our minds and hearts.

Of course, if my lifelong experience is any general indication, many of us don't even know where the override button is. But then, perhaps, we have never tried to find it. If we think walking in the shadows is in some way beneficial or if we enjoy feeling sorry for ourselves and are afraid to stretch, we will never change.

Looking back, I think I must have seen some advantage in keeping to those shadows. From my university studies in psychology, I understood the currently popular "cognitive theories," which claim that we all have personal power to rise above our circumstances, to supersede our "personal programming." I also knew that the gospel tells us that we are free to choose (see 2 Nephi 2:27). Nevertheless, I didn't know how to use, or didn't want to use, those teachings to think optimistically. Any contrary event, no matter how small, became the focus of discouraging, disparaging thoughts and such negative pursuits as: assigning blame, wallowing in self-pity, and feeling resentful, all of which are a part of a continuous downward spiral.

I remember one Christmas season when, as usual, I had been trying to run faster than I had strength. My December days in that era were often filled with too many events and self-imposed responsibilities. Red and green were the colors of exhaustion, not the colors of joy; and that particular year I was more weary than usual. While we were visiting Salt Lake City, my husband and daughter spontaneously decided to go to Temple Square, and I trudged along without enthusiasm, resenting the intrusion, murmuring about the bitter-cold night, wishing I were at home curled up with a blanket and a good book.

After stepping into Temple Square, we wandered through the scenes of Christmas, gazed at the millions of multicolored lights, listened to carols being sung by community choirs, and took a walk up the ramp in the North Visitor's Center to see the majestic Christus statue.

Although my eyes and ears told me everything was lovely, I still felt nothing. I might have generated holiday joy through my testimony of the truth and beauty of Christmas, but I chose not to do so.

Then, before leaving the Square, we stopped to look at the life-size nativity scene located on the snow-covered plaza between the historic Tabernacle and the visitor's center. I was awed, as I always am, at how the lighted Christus —from behind the glistening floor-to-ceiling windows of the building—dominates the locale. For a few minutes I gazed on the beauty of the setting, then, hearing the Christmas story beginning to be told over the speaker system, turned back to the manger scene.

Several seconds later my eyes were drawn again to the Christus, and, two or three times, I visually traveled the distance from the manger to the statue of the resurrected Jesus and back again, witnessing in that panorama a time line. First, at the manger, His birth. Then, between the nativity scene and the Christus, thirty-three years of mortality brimming with miracles and teachings concluding with the incomprehensible pain in Gethsemane, betrayal, and crucifixion. Finally, back at the Christus, I saw the grandeur of the triumphant Christ and beheld a vision of eternity.

None of this doctrine and history was new to me, but seeing all of it compressed into the scene before me provided a new sense of the tremendous meaning of the Savior's being. To get a better perspective, I stepped away from my family and the crowd.

In the scene at the stable I saw peace, but the power was in the time line. Without the time line, we have no reason to celebrate His birth. If we forget the time line, the manger has no message. On the other hand, when we remember the time line, the joy of Christmas can last all year long.

In the words of Isaiah, the entire time line was evident, suddenly more significant than ever before: "For unto us a child is born, unto us a son is given: and the government shall be upon his shoulder: and his name shall be called Wonderful, Counsellor, The mighty God, The everlasting Father, The Prince of Peace" (Isaiah 9:6).

What a night it must have been, I thought, that night when angels sang, shepherds knelt, and a new star appeared—a night when a baby was born who would, in thirty-three short years, bring to pass an eternal time line, not only for Himself, but for everyone.

When the Christmas presentation came to an end, my thoughts were very far away. I was surprised to find that my family was freezing and in a hurry to leave.

For me, the temperature had changed. The evening felt warm and the season felt lovely.

That particular Christmas, I had built a wall between myself and joy. I needed a little Temple Square magic to level the barricade and let in the light. I could have enjoyed the season from beginning to end if only I'd had access to a "lemonade recipe." Unfortunately, in those days I possessed no such formula, not at Christmas time nor in any other season. The Temple Square magic of that year was short-lived because I didn't realize I had the power to take the initiative and consistently challenge negative interference, even though a model had always been close by.

The Mormon pioneers made their pathway bright on a regular basis in spite of all their burdens and trials. They understood that joy is as much a part of the gospel as endurance. They eliminated blame, self-pity, and resentment with the attitude expressed in their all-time great lemonade song, "Come, Come, Ye Saints" (*Hymns*, no. 30). They talked and sang themselves into the sunshine.

> Come, come, ye Saints, no toil nor labor fear;
> But with joy wend your way.
> Though hard to you this journey may appear,
> Grace shall be as your day.
> 'Tis better far for us to strive
> Our useless cares from us to drive;

Do this, and joy your hearts will swell—
All is well! All is well!

Why should we mourn or think our lot is hard?
'Tis not so; all is right.
Why should we think to earn a great reward
If we now shun the fight?
Gird up your loins; fresh courage take.
Our God will never us forsake;
And soon we'll have this tale to tell—
All is well! All is well!

The heartfelt message of this optimistic pioneer song is to constantly think of good things and rejoice, and the last verse provides an extra spoonful of sugar. No matter what might happen in their future, whether they died or whether they lived, they would find a way to make lemonade.

And should we die before our journey's through,
Happy day! All is well!
We then are free from toil and sorrow, too;
With the just we shall dwell!
But if our lives are spared again
To see the Saints their rest obtain,
Oh, how we'll make this chorus swell—
All is well! All is well!

So much of optimism is in talking ourselves out of the bad and into the good, taking personal responsibility to create sunshine and mix lemonade, in searching for the sugar and doing so consistently, without delay. The scriptures teach us that "Hope deferred maketh the heart sick" (Proverbs 13:12).

Having finally seen the light and tasted the sweetness of real lemonade, Brazilian style, I knew there was no refreshment, no magic, in the shadows. Analyzing the 4-point recipe for making lemonade, I was sure it would consistently yield the desired results, but I was equally certain that I needed to keep the recipe close by and garner the courage to use it when the lemons' fall would demand *true grit*.

When a dark "May night" descends, finding the flags, the confetti, the rose petals, the energy and the will to scatter sunshine can be a superhuman task. Yet we can do it! We can mix lemonade, even in the dark, and thereby ensure that "joy cometh in the morning" (Psalm 30:5).

The sun will shine upon us and from us when we give ourselves a push in the right direction.

"CAREFUL AND TROUBLED"

Eventually I began to wonder why it had taken me so long to learn the sunshine principles, why I needed such an awesome fountain of lemonade to understand the recipe. After much introspection, I discovered the missing ingredient. It turned out to be spontaneity. I lacked that sunshine ability to turn on a dime, change horses in midstream, be impromptu or extemporaneous, or to act on the spur-of-the-moment.

Spontaneity is not something that fosters perpetual party-time and continual "fun stuff." Neither is it impulsiveness or impetuousness—darting off in any and all directions without purpose or discretion. Also, it is not an unconscious or mechanical behavior. Instead, spontaneity is sudden action "controlled or directed internally" and "occurring or seeming to occur in the natural course of things" (*Webster's Third New International Dictionary Unabridged*, Volume III, Merriam Webster, Inc., 1986, 2204).

Spontaneity provides instantaneous momentum, which helps us deal effectively with life's surprises.

As a "perfectionist," my ability to adjust to change was just about nonexistent. Once I put a plan in motion, I would see it through to the end, no matter what. Completion of any task was high on my list of priorities, even if the task itself wasn't a priority; even if the task had become a useless endeavor; even if life required something else. That's why careful Martha of the New Testament had so often come to save me. She, too, apparently lacked spontaneity; but Jesus, understanding her weakness, offered kindly correction.

> Now it came to pass, as they went, that he entered into a certain village: and a certain woman named Martha received him into her house.
>
> And she had a sister called Mary, which also sat at Jesus' feet, and heard his word.
>
> But Martha was cumbered about much serving, and came to him, and said, Lord, dost thou not care that my sister hath left me to serve alone? bid her therefore that she help me.
>
> And Jesus answered and said unto her, Martha, Martha, thou art careful and troubled about many things:
>
> But one thing is needful: and Mary hath chosen that good part, which shall not be taken away from her (Luke 10:38–42).

When "Martha" came to visit me the first time, my husband was serving as president of the Spain Seville Mission, and, in spite of my dislike of anything resembling culinary chores, I had concluded that my lot was to be "Keeper of the

Kitchen." As such, I decided that whatever missionaries enjoyed eating, I was obligated to prepare.

As a result of this faulty reasoning about my responsibilities, I soon found myself little more than a slave to the stove.

As the months came and went, so did arriving missionaries, departing missionaries, zone leaders' conferences, sisters' meetings, office staff meetings, official visitors, etc. These occasions always found me cooking and resenting that aspect of my calling. It never crossed my mind that I could change my attitude by simply retracting my commitment to the kitchen.

Then, thumbing through some old files one day, I came across a talk I had once given. The talk began with a scripture, one of my favorite scriptures, the story of careful and troubled Martha.

As I read again the description of that brief but significant event, I stopped short, for in my mind's eye the Martha of the story was me. I tried to shake off the image without success. I feigned lack of comprehension, but finally I had to admit that I was indeed "cumbered about much serving."

And the Spirit whispered: "You've neglected your guests and your family. You've become a complainer. Your job is to be an example, not a cook. Yes, the missionaries deserve all good things, but you need not exhaust yourself. They devour anything edible. You need to simplify!"

That very day I changed course, and the burden was lifted.

Unfortunately, however, I didn't generalize the lesson. I

continued being careful and troubled about many other things, resenting interruptions and imperfections, charging on to task completion, unable to spontaneously change gears.

A few years later the perfectionist streak in me again mounted a *coup d'etat* and took charge of my life. I decided I needed to put my house in order.

I cleaned closets and moved furniture.

I filed and sorted papers, clothes, and food storage.

I brought photo albums and slide trays up to date.

I organized recipes and church and work supplies.

I wrote letters, adding and subtracting names and addresses from the correspondence book as I went along.

I updated journals and books of remembrance.

I went shopping for odds and ends: a desk lamp, TV trays, a new frying pan.

I was on a nonstop march toward perfect organization (with the exception of those things that perfection must march around: my husband's desk and my daughter's room); and wonder of wonders, I arrived.

I surveyed the immaculate house and peacefully peered into perfectly ordered closets and tidy drawers. I admired the neatly stacked papers and files. I rejoiced that my projects were all done. I crossed off the last item on my pending list, crumpled it up, and tossed it away. I had met my goal, and I breathed a well-deserved sigh of relief. The war was over—or at least I thought it was—until the next morning arrived. Then I found that "perfection" liked being captain of my soul and did not want to relinquish power. The commander had become a dictator, and logic was nowhere to be found.

For more than a week I organized and straightened things that didn't need to be organized or straightened. I looked for projects to do, and, when I couldn't find any, I invented some. I wrote new lists: things to do at Christmas, things to do in the summer, things to do in the year 2010. I kept trying to perfect that which was already sufficiently perfect until one day I opened my scriptures and, once again, found myself face-to-face with Martha.

"Perfection" immediately loosened its grip, and I concluded that I might often find myself "cumbered about" and "careful and troubled." It was one of my weaknesses. I wanted things done right, done my way, planned in advance. I wanted life to dance to my music. But, of course, life has its own plans, its own music. My perspective was a formula for discouragement and stress, not for lemonade and sunshine.

Then, in spite of my intention to remain uninvolved in the events, I ran headlong into that magic, spontaneous, Brazilian day. If I were ever going to wring all the good out of life, I would obviously have to trade my cautious, careful, and troubled nature for at least a dash of spontaneity.

Spontaneity is essential to finding sunshine on the crooked, rocky road of mortality because that road is so very unpredictable. Each turn brings surprises. If we suddenly find an unexpected obstacle but are unwilling to make the necessary course corrections, the trip quickly becomes a snarl of confusion. To find adventure in the unexpected, new vistas in the change of scenery, and lessons in alternate routes is to find spontaneity and sunshine. Adopting spontaneity allows us to respond to each circumstance, each event, each moment in time appropriately—to respond naturally to the context of each situation.

Sister Janet Lee relates the story of her daughter, Stephanie, who was told as she entered her kindergarten room for the first time to choose her favorite color crayon from a box and write her name. Although Stephanie knew how to write her name, she "stood still, staring blankly at the box of crayons with her knees locked and hands behind her back." When a second request for Stephanie to choose a crayon and write her name elicited no response, the teacher said, "That's okay. We will help you learn to write your name . . ."

Sister Lee later asked Stephanie why she had not written her name. Stephanie replied, "I couldn't. The teacher said to choose my favorite color, and there wasn't a pink crayon in the box!" ("Choices and Challenges," *Ensign*, Feb. 1995, 59).

Stephanie rounded a corner, came face-to-face with an obstacle, and was unable to make a spur-of-the-moment adjustment.

Children, fortunately, have natural resilience. They may realize that expectations cannot be met, but they don't build walls as a result. On the other hand, when confronted with unpleasant situations or necessary attitude and behavior changes, adults can be so bound by habits, traditions, and expectations that rearranging priorities results in anger, resentment, complaints, and a view of lemons falling all around. What's more, they haven't a clue where to find a recipe for lemonade. Instead, they sag under the weight of the chip on their shoulder and wilt in the darkness caused by their ever-present walls. Immovable "pink-crayon" people are hard on themselves and hard on others. They sometimes even take God to task for not ensuring the availability of their preferred color.

Martha and I and all other careful and troubled "pink-crayon" people respond to circumstances based on plans and expectations instead of listening to our conscience, intuition, and the Spirit, and doing what is appropriate in each particular situation. Careful and troubled people have a problem managing time by context, a principle taught in the scriptures:

> To every thing there is a season, and a time to every purpose under the heaven:
> A time to be born, and a time to die; a time to plant, and a time to pluck up that which is planted;
> A time to kill, and a time to heal; a time to break down, and a time to build up;
> A time to weep, and a time to laugh; a time to mourn, and a time to dance;
> A time to cast away stones, and a time to gather stones together; a time to embrace, and a time to refrain from embracing;
> A time to get, and a time to lose; a time to keep, and a time to cast away;
> A time to rend, and a time to sew; a time to keep silence, and a time to speak;
> A time to love, and a time to hate; a time of war, and a time of peace (Ecclesiastes 3:1-8).

And there's a time to enjoy roses and a time to see the beauty of dandelions. A time to plan for a Porsche and a time to praise the local bus system. A time to create some space between you and others who would destroy and a time to draw a circle of love. There's a time to hold on and a time to let go, a time to follow the plan and a time to be spontaneous. If the time has come to make lemonade, to look at things differently, change plans, push the "override button," buy some sugar! Embrace gratitude, hope, and love.

People who are capable of being appropriately spontaneous allow themselves room to move. They can go in search of sunshine and sugar, even in the dark, for their flashlight is always handy. They can stop to study, to pray, to relax. They can get up and go, to create, to play, to serve. They know when it's time to plan and measure every move and when it's better to take the risk and "go for it." They sense when they should maintain the status quo and when it's time for spontaneity. What's more, they shift gears cheerfully, willing to juggle the consequences.

At times there is a need for spontaneity, as obstacles and detours cross our paths one after another. In other moments our agendas, plans, and expectations move along at the speed of light without interruption. However, refusing to adjust our plans in the face of changing situations obscures the possibility of sunshine.

For careful and troubled creatures of habit, even knowing the value of spontaneity does not eliminate uneasiness, for there is intuition, instinct, and guesswork implied, which means the results are uncertain. That lack of a written agenda can be frightening to those of us who cling tightly to plans and programs, but we must remember that staying with invalid contracts can be even more chancy. We can be wrong just by refusing to adapt.

That we will have to adapt to change is one of the few constants in life. As mortals, we are not still-life artists, putting permanent images on our canvases. In fact, life resembles a jigsaw puzzle more than a painting, and it isn't always possible to figure out in advance where all the pieces go and then sequentially complete the scene. Instead, we must keep trying new pieces, learning how they fit into a constantly changing flow of events. Instinct and intuition help as we work our way through the maze of life, which sometimes calls for patience and sometimes requires that we move energetically ahead. When surprises present themselves, it helps if we can respond with spontaneity.

Brazil's Ayrton Senna, who understood the value of spontaneity and was equal parts racing driver and psychologist/philosopher, had his own puzzle analogy: "You position the pieces, imagining how you're going to put them together, but then someone comes and mixes them up, and you need to start over again."

From such a bewildering challenge comes the need for spontaneity. If the worst happens, we can then regroup and begin anew.

Used wisely, spontaneity is the spice of life. This the eccentrics understand. They know that a day without spontaneity is like a day without sunshine!

A DASH OF
SPONTANEITY

Perhaps spontaneity became such an essential component of sunshine for me because I had lived without it for so long, at least for as long as I can remember. But in that past time, now temporarily forgotten, we must have all possessed it. Then, we all "shouted for joy" (Job 38:7) at the prospect of mortality, even though becoming mortal would require an abrupt adjustment to circumstances we had never before experienced.

Amidst the joy, therefore, we might have been apprehensive about the uncertainties that would be involved. In response to those concerns, Satan proposed a plan that would eliminate any choices in mortality. In doing so, he sought to "destroy the agency of man" (Moses 4:3). Satan and his followers wanted an enclosed harbor; one without waves, where there would be no possibility of failure or the potential for adventure. His plan would not only eliminate choice but also learning experiences, spontaneity, and joy.

When we distanced ourselves from him by choosing to follow our Father in Heaven and His Beloved Son, we possessed something that gave us strength to step into the unknown, to attempt the untried. Thus it is that "we walk by faith, not by sight" (2 Corinthians 5:7).

It is by faith that we conquer any fears, for faith vanquishes doubt and propels action, as explained in *Lectures on Faith:*

"If men were duly to consider themselves, and turn their thoughts and reflections to the operation of their own minds, they would readily discover that it is faith, and faith only, which is the moving cause of all action in them; that without it both mind and body would be in a state of inactivity, and all their exertions would cease, both physical and mental" (*Lectures on Faith* 1:10).

Therefore, it was faith that allowed us to shout for joy in our premortal life, and it is faith that will again give us the power to proclaim our joy over and over again in mortality. We believe the first principle of the gospel is faith in the Lord Jesus Christ (see Articles of Faith 1:4).

In that former time, we shouted joyfully because we were excited to have the opportunity for eternal progression and because we had faith that Jesus could and would do all He promised to do. By making us perfect through the power of the Atonement, He would make it possible for us to return to our heavenly home. We will give that same joyful shout in mortality when we understand the all-encompassing nature of His mission.

When I first began to grasp the importance of spontaneity, I thought I understood. I had taught the principles of the mission of Christ over and over again.

I understood that through the Resurrection, He saves us

from physical death. "For as in Adam all die, even so in Christ shall all be made alive" (1 Corinthians 15:22). The glorious promise is that because of Christ, we will all be resurrected—meaning our spirits and bodies will be reunited eternally—no matter how righteous or wicked we have been in mortality.

I also understood that Jesus will save us from the effects of our sins. When we repent and cease any repetition of those behaviors, they will disappear completely, without a trace. Isaiah explained this marvelous principle when he said, "[T]hough your sins be as scarlet, they shall be as white as snow; though they be red like crimson, they shall be as wool" (Isaiah 1:18). And in a wonderfully comforting, latter-day revelation, the Lord, himself, said "Behold, he who has repented of his sins, the same is forgiven, and I, the Lord, remember them no more" (D&C 58:42).

I knew that through obedience to the laws and ordinances of the gospel, we will become the children of Christ. In the sense that we are reborn in Him, we become Christ's sons and daughters. "And now, because of the covenant which ye have made ye shall be called the children of Christ, his sons, and his daughters; for behold, this day he hath spiritually begotten you; for ye say that your hearts are changed through faith on his name; therefore, ye are born of him and have become his sons and his daughters" (Mosiah 5:7).

I understood that no matter how hard we try, we cannot do everything we want to or be all we want to be or should be. We fall below the ideal in every way. We need

Jesus to provide for us what we don't have, to make up the difference, as Brother Stephen E. Robinson explains: "We all want something desperately, . . . We want the kingdom of God. We want to go home to our heavenly parents worthy and clean [but] at some point in our spiritual progress, we realize what the full price of admission into that kingdom is, and we also realize that we cannot pay it. . . . At that point, the Savior steps in and says, 'So you've done all you can do, but it's not enough. Well, don't despair. . . . How much *do* you have? How much *can* fairly be expected of you? You give me exactly that much . . . and do all you *can* do, and I will provide the rest'" (*Believing Christ* [1992], 32–33).

Though we may have only a tiny bit to give, it will be enough, if we have in addition a broken heart and a contrite spirit. When we, knowing our weaknesses, trust in Him and put our hand in His, He will make up the difference and usher us back into the presence of our Father, thus ending that separation called spiritual death.

I also knew there is an obligation on my part, to do all I can do and endure to the end. "Wherefore, if ye shall press forward, feasting upon the word of Christ, and endure to the end, behold, thus saith the Father: Ye shall have eternal life" (2 Nephi 31:20).

I knew that to endure means to remain faithful, to choose the right.

To do all I could do. To choose the right. Somehow I had interpreted those principles as: "Live life cautiously. Be careful and troubled. Make a move only when you're sure and feel guilty afterward if the move was in the wrong direction." I wanted the locations for all the pieces to my puzzle to be determined in advance, and woe be unto anyone trying to mix up my plans. I resented any interference in the calm harbor of my comfort zone where, though the sky was somewhat gray, the scenery was familiar and the water was crystal clear. In the harbor, I knew exactly what to expect. I just didn't realize there is a whole ocean bathed in sunshine waiting to be discovered. Its name is "Spontaneity."

But there was a day, a day of truth and light that grew out of that magic Brazilian day and was linked tightly to the lessons on love, lemonade, and spontaneity. On that day I realized I was completely free to travel, to turn on a dime, to change horses in midstream, be impromptu and extemporaneous, and to act on the spur-of-the-moment. I could relax and be myself and not allow any fear of failure or of pointing fingers to act upon me and impede my progress. When I finally accepted the jigsaw puzzle nature and the uncertainty of mortality, I shouted for joy.

Mortality is a practice field where we are to learn new skills, develop wholesome character traits, and live gospel principles. As we practice we will often make mistakes. Orson F. Whitney referred to such mistakes as "blunders" when he said: "[Man] sins when he does the opposite of what he knows to be right. Up to that point he only blunders. One may suffer painful consequences for only blundering, but he cannot commit sin unless he knows better than to do the thing in which the sin consists" (Bruce R. McConkie, *Mormon Doctrine*, 2nd edition [1979], 735).

The scriptures clarify the important difference between mistakes and sins. "[I]nasmuch as they erred it might be made known; . . . And inasmuch as they sinned they might be chastened, that they might repent" (D&C 1:25, 27).

Elder Dallin H. Oaks explains: "Both sins and mistakes can hurt us and both require attention, but the scriptures direct a different treatment. Chewing on a live electrical cord or diving headfirst into water of uncertain depth are mistakes that should be made known so that they can be avoided. Violations of the commandments of God are sins that require chastening and repentance. In the treatment process we should not require repentance for mistakes, but we are commanded to preach the necessity of repentance for sins" ("Sins and Mistakes," *Ensign*, Oct. 1996, 62).

Though we must avoid sin and repent as needed, mistakes are different. They are the result of our mortal inexperience. We don't know how to do everything. We need to learn academic skills, social skills, business skills, parenting skills, just to name a few; and in the process we have to take a few chances and risk a few failures. When we err we need correction, much of which can be self-imposed.

The desire to do it all perfectly or not do it at all is never a mortal option, although careful and troubled people often try to make it one. We constantly take ourselves (and others) to task for just being human.

Accepting the limits of our mortality, while not using mortality as an excuse for unwise conduct, is vitally important if mortality is to play its full role in "the great plan of happiness" (Alma 42:8). Unrealistic expectations never lead to joy. "Mistakes are inevitable in the process of growth in mortality. To avoid all possibility of error is to avoid all possibility of growth. In the parable of the talents, the Savior told of a servant who was so anxious to minimize the risk of loss through a mistaken investment that he hid up his talent and did nothing with it. That servant was condemned by his master" (see Matthew 25:24–30; Oaks, *op. cit.*, 67).

The servants of that parable were each given different stewardships or talents—sums of money—to manage. All of us, likewise, have different stewardships—lives to improve. Mortality is a good gift, a remarkable gift. The parable of the talents is about making a good gift better. Some have a large gift, some have a small gift, but on all of us rests the responsibility to enlarge the gift.

While serving in a foreign country, the wife of a mission president was approached by a sister of humble circumstances. The sister was a new convert and was overwhelmed by the appearance and abilities of the mission president's wife. Near tears, she queried: "How can I ever hope to gain all the eternal rewards? I will never be like you."

Recognizing her own personal inadequacies, and near tears herself, the wife of the mission president replied, "I have a little more experience, but you still have skills I don't have. Each of us is learning, and all of us are okay as we learn."

We *are* okay as we learn. That *is* the joy of mortality.

And it is so because of Jesus! When we cannot find sunshine we may be "looking beyond the mark," searching for answers somewhere outside the core of the gospel: Jesus Christ and his mission. "Adam fell that men might be; and men are, that they might have joy. And the Messiah cometh in the fulness of time, that he may redeem the children of men from the fall. And because that they are redeemed from the fall they have become free forever, knowing good from evil; to act for themselves and not to be acted upon" (2 Nephi 2:25–26).

That we must use mortality as a practice field is a result of the Fall. That we are free to do so is a gift of the Atonement. Jesus provides a safety net for us, to rescue us from sin, from weakness, and from mortal limitations, even from everyday spontaneous blunders. "We can learn by experience, even from our innocent and inevitable mistakes, and our Savior will help us carry the burden of the afflictions that are inevitable in mortality" (Oaks, *op. cit.*, 67).

Throughout my life I had been so much like the third servant in the parable of the talents, trying to minimize the possibility of error, refusing to take a risk or to trust the safety net to work in my behalf. Hiding in our comfort zones, restricting our progress, recoiling from the various colors of crayons that life spontaneously offers is a result of fear, not faith, and is in opposition to the great plan of happiness.

Adam and Eve felt the euphoria of freedom when they were taught the totality of Christ's mission: "[A]s thou hast fallen thou mayest be redeemed, and all mankind, even as many as will. And in that day Adam blessed God and was filled, and began to prophesy concerning all the families of the earth, saying: Blessed be the name of God, for because of my transgression my eyes are opened, and in this life I shall have joy, and again in the flesh I shall see God. And Eve, his wife, heard all these things and was glad, saying: Were it not for our transgression we never should have had seed, and never should have known good and evil, and the joy of our redemption, and the eternal life which God giveth unto all the obedient" (Moses 5:9–11).

It is not by coincidence that the famous scripture on joy, "men are, that they might have joy," is followed immediately by the doctrine of the Atonement, "And the Messiah cometh in the fulness of time, that he may redeem the children of men from the fall" (2 Nephi 2:25–26).

When I finally understood that all of us are covered by the Atonement even in small learning experiences, I shouted for joy as "careful and troubled" gave way to "peace" and "spontaneity."

Not too long thereafter, I was surprised when I calmly gave a talk extemporaneously. I was startled when I found myself laughing easily at bumbling bureaucracy. I was astonished when I made a visible human error without feeling guilty. I was amazed when I discovered myself singing in the rain. I was speechless when I left a task unfinished without any regret. I was shocked when I ascertained that life is at least as funny as it is frustrating. And when, one day, I found the pieces to my puzzle all jumbled, I was flabbergasted that I wished no woe on anyone or anything. I was learning to accept the variables, the detours, and myself.

Why had I spent my life hiding the real me, assuming I needed to be someone more perfect, when the truth made living so easy, so joyful? Ayrton Senna put it this way: "The main thing is to be yourself and not allow people to disturb you, to be different because they want you to be different. You've got to be yourself. Many times you [make] a mistake due to your own personality, or your own character, or interferences that you get on the way, but you learn, and the main thing is to make sure you learn through your mistakes and get better."

If the talk I gave spontaneously was less than perfect, if laughing and singing were somehow out of place, if the task I had left undone should have been completed, and if the new "puzzle" challenge created more adventure in self-correction, peace still survived. I knew I had a safety net and could act for myself. I was truly free to "learn . . . and get better."

In that long ago time, when all of us shouted for joy, I'm sure we did so spontaneously, out of feelings of profound gratitude and faith. We would leave the harbor with infinite protection.

Realizing how blessed we are, how free we are through the love and sacrifice of Jesus Christ to sail the seven seas in search of truth and progress, to strive to improve our gift, increase our stewardship, and still remain safe in the arms of His love is the source of permanent sunshine.

Joy is never-ending when we realize how much God loves the world.

FLAGS AND
REFLECTIONS

.

After that magic Brazilian day, I thought a lot about the need we all have to feel important and loved. Giving others a belief in themselves is one of the greatest gifts, something we can do with very few tools and little time. To accept equally the value of all the children of our Father in Heaven and to let them know we care is to practice unconditional love.

Ayrton Senna was not a political figure, not a military leader, not a religious guide. He was just a well-known, successful Brazilian who consistently brightened the pathway for his countrymen. He took every opportunity to communicate his conviction that determination, faith, and love make all things possible.

As a result of his charisma, the TV audience for Formula 1 races grew in Brazil to staggering proportions. The people loved him, and because of his skills, they knew there was always a likely chance that Senna would win. When he did, he would pull to the sidelines before beginning his victory lap, take a Brazilian flag from the hand of a delighted spectator, and then round the track with that green, yellow, and blue banner flying high. In those moments, *because* of those moments, his countrymen flew on his wings.

When he died, various commentators tried to capture the essence of his influence in observations such as these:

He gave to the country a lesson in self-esteem. Literally, he saved the nation ("E, No Ultimo Dia, O Guerreiro Repousou,"—And, at the Last Day, the Warrior Rested, *Revista Manchete*, 6 May 1995, center poster).

He offered love for Brazil in such a way that his success inspired an expression of ability for the country (Tasso Jereissati, "Guardemos o Piloto como se Guarda um Tesouro,"—We Keep the Racing-Driver as One Would Keep a Treasure, *Folha de São Paulo*, April 23, 1995, 4/8).

He, an antenna of feelings, transmitted and captured again a healthy pride in being Brazilian (*Ibid.*).

He brought within him and communicated to all of us the certainty of victory ("Ayrton Senna Special," concluding text by Michel Laurence, *TV Cultura*, São Paulo, May 1, 1995).

A simple flag, a sincere message, a gift of sunshine. Some people seem to know instinctively that the worth of souls is great (see D&C 18:10) and that each of us has a responsibility to proclaim their value.

You can make the pathway bright,
Fill the soul with heaven's light . . .
(*Hymns*, no. 228)

When people feel important and loved, their pathway shines and their soul glows.

On a *New Era* "Mormonad" of a few years ago, there was pictured a green speckled frog with protruding eyes. The little fellow is crouched on a damp lily pad obviously waiting for the next unsuspecting bug. He is a frog just like any other frog except that perched on his flat little head, between those two bulging eyes, is a tiny red and gold crown. The picture has a caption: "There aren't any FROGS—just handsome PRINCES who don't know who they are."

Or, it might have said, "have FORGOTTEN" who they are!

To repeat: We are "sons and daughters, children of a King" (*Hymns*, no. 249). We are royalty! Or rephrased, "I am a child of God" (*Hymns*, no. 301). Or again: "Ye are gods; and all of you are children of the most High" (Psalm 82:6).

Each child of God, no matter his or her circumstances, always has maximum value. Each was worth the high and terrible price of the Atonement. "For God so loved the world, that he gave his only begotten Son" (John 3:16).

The world is us, you and me, the regular folks; and they, too, the heroes and the villains, past, present, and future.

59

No matter our station or their station in life, we and they are of infinite worth.

As children of our Father in Heaven, we are loved by Him in the only way His perfection allows Him to love us: perfectly, unconditionally. This means that He loves us always, under all circumstances. His love does not increase or decrease as a result of who we are, how we look, what we have, or what we do. He knows our potential as well as our weaknesses, and even when we are far from being all we should be, He still loves us completely.

Because of our infinite worth, our divine nature, we have the power to do something about our behavior—to modify, change, achieve a higher level. Because we are royalty we can, little by little, improve everything we do.

But too many of us see the inverse. We think that our weaknesses and failings reduce our value. That false premise is a lie from Satan, who has no sunshine in his heart. He wants us to be miserable, to focus on life's struggles and setbacks, to feel less than regal, sometimes even see ourselves as green speckled frogs. Without the sunshine of personal worth, we can forget who we are and become discouraged at our lack of success, become disappointed at the inability to locate our "gifts," or dismayed at the face looking back at us from the mirror. Too often we forget that we are royalty!

When we understand and accept our value, understand and accept that we are royalty even if we sometimes fail to act like princes and princesses, we will discover a self-confidence that will empower us to improve. We will always feed ourselves words of faith and encouragement.

An expectation that we must achieve mortal perfection can be a major impediment to our acquiring this sunshine. If we insist on being perfect, if we demand perfection of others, if we insist that life work perfectly in order to be acceptable, the light will go out. Although we must stretch, even struggle against the odds, we should not break in the process.

Elder Russell M. Nelson has explained that the word *perfection* as used in the scriptures would be better rendered *whole* or *complete*, "to reach a distant end, to be fully developed, to consummate or to finish" (*Ensign*, Nov. 1995, 86). *Perfection* defined as being "absolutely correct" is an inaccurate interpretation of the word, for we cannot make ourselves absolutely correct—not now, not in eternity. For us, perfection is not an achievement. It is an inheritance we will receive after we have demonstrated our willingness to be obedient to the prerequisite laws and ordinances of the gospel.

Moroni explained how this works when he taught, "Yea, come unto Christ, and be perfected in him, and deny yourselves of all ungodliness; and if ye shall deny yourselves of all ungodliness, and love God with all your might, mind and strength, then is his grace sufficient for you, that by his grace ye may be perfect in Christ" (Moroni 10:32).

Perfection is a gift from Christ to His disciples. Ether 12:27 puts our current circumstances in perspective: "And if men come unto me I will show unto them their weakness. I give unto men weakness that they may be humble; and my grace is sufficient for all men that humble themselves before me; for if they humble themselves before me, and have faith in me, then will I make weak things become strong unto them."

Our mortality will not be burdensome when we understand that one of its purposes is to cause us to strengthen our relationship with our Father and His Son as we turn to Them for help with our specific problems. Because of Their unconditional love, They will always be waiting.

Much of the Savior's teaching to us has to do with love, unconditional love, for we are instructed to become like Him (see 3 Nephi 27:27). According to His words, we need to learn to avoid contention, to forgive men their trespasses, to love our enemies, to cease judging the weaknesses of others, to control anger, and become reconciled to our fellowmen (see 3 Nephi 11–14). Too often as mortals we love conditionally, with strings attached. We love based on the appearances, abilities, achievements, attitudes, and general behavior of our fellowmen. The Lord knows this. "[T]he Lord seeth not as man seeth; for man looketh on the outward appearance, but the Lord looketh on the heart" (1 Sam. 16:7).

Nevertheless, He challenges us to change. "Love one another; as I have loved you" (John 13:34).

We can begin that metamorphosis by seeing the infinite worth and potential of each child of God. We can stop pointing fingers. We can cease building "walls." We can let others know we care.

Ayrton Senna was one who knew how to scatter the sunshine of personal worth, at home and away. There was in his life a lack of walls, which, at least in part, accounts for his universal appeal and why his picture appeared on the cover of *TIME International* the week after he died (May 16, 1994, no. 20). With regard to people and relationships, he possessed a genuine tenderness that was in stark contrast to his intense determination on a race track. Some people were perplexed by this polarity in his personality, but most were both exhilarated by his professional aggressiveness and warmed by his personal gentleness. Men admired him. Women loved him. Most of all, children worshipped him.

At the time he died, before I knew very much about him, I was especially amazed by the Brazilian children's reaction to his death. Brazilian children of every age and social level were so profoundly affected that they seemed unable to focus on studying, playing, or even sleeping. Classrooms turned into counseling centers the week he died, and the children made posters, wrote letters, and sang songs about him. On the day of his burial, schools were closed.

Through it all, I couldn't help but ask myself what created the incredible bond between Senna and the children. With a little research I found the answer, an answer I should have been able to guess: Ayrton *loved the children*. He could captivate just one child or an entire room full with his genuine interest and belief in them. Always their advocate, he defined a child as "the symbol of life, of family, of the present and of the future. A human being without sin" (Ney Bianchi, "Confidencias a Beira de Morte,"—Confidences at the Edge of Death, *Revista Manchete*, 6 May 1995, 20).

Not surprisingly, the children fell completely under his spell.

The bond between them was firmly cemented a few months before his death when he introduced a cartoon character named Senninha (Little Senna). This little racing champion bore an obvious resemblance to his namesake; and the children were delighted that Ayrton not only cared about them but, through Senninha, also consented to be numbered among them.

In Senninha's adventures, Ayrton shared his belief that any true victory, on or off a racetrack, is a result of education, determination, hard work, good deeds, friendship, and love. Although he is no longer physically present, he still speaks through Senninha—even to a new generation.

On that magic day in May the children mourned the most but they also waved their flags the highest, in tribute and farewell to their best friend. Ayrton gave them a sense of their true worth, and there are children in Brazil who will live their whole lives and never, ever forget.

Because Ayrton Senna seemed to be so conscious of the worth of souls, thinking of him as a friend was easy for most people, not just for the children, not just for Brazilians. Although Brazil claimed the major portion of Ayrton Senna's heart, there was room for so much more.

On that tragic Formula 1 weekend—on the day before Senna's death, on the same track in Italy—the first Formula 1 fatality in twelve years occurred when rookie Austrian driver, Roland Ratzenberger, was killed in a crash during qualifying trials.

Senna, who had never been seriously injured and never seen anyone die in all his years in racing, was stunned. Many took note of his tears before he finally retreated from the track in solitude to mourn.

Later, when the business of racing continued virtually uninterrupted, Senna sadly concluded that if his fallen comrade was to be honored, he would have to do it himself. For Ayrton, Roland Ratzenberger, though just a rookie, was of great worth. Senna, therefore, committed to do everything possible to win the race the following day; but, this one time, his homeland would have to forgive the absence of the green, yellow, and blue banner on the victory lap. This one time he would raise an Austrian flag.

That intended tribute to Roland Ratzenberger died with Ayrton Senna. Nevertheless, the story of Senna's plans—confirmed by the discovery of a furled Austrian flag in the remains of his car—quickly became legend: A résumé, many thought, of Senna's life.

When, in retrospect, I examined the life of Ayrton Senna, I discovered why he was able to transmit so much sunshine to others. He believed resolutely in himself. Though realistic about his personal weaknesses and limitations and always willing to learn and change, he possessed unconditional self-assurance and self-acceptance. Even when he slipped, he knew he could get a good foothold and climb again. The melody of "I Am a Child of God" would not have been familiar to him, but he was a prayerful student of the Bible. He recognized his value and potential and the value and potential of others. Gentle words and deeds were a staple of his life.

On 21 March 1995 (the date when Ayrton would have turned 35 years of age), as I was watching a nostalgic Senna news clip on television, one of his gentle moments reached out across time to send me a personal message.

The moment was embedded in a short collage of his life and showed a delighted Senna on the winner's podium in Adelaide, Australia, in November 1993. The year had not been his best (he placed second in the overall standings); but he was grateful to have won this last race of the season, the last race he would drive for the team he had been affiliated with for six years. In 1994 he would move to a new team.

The Adelaide win would also be his last racing victory.

In the scene—beside Senna and slightly below him on the second place podium—stood French driver, Alain Prost, who had won the driver's championship for 1993 and was retiring from racing. Prost and Senna had once been companions on the same team, a difficult union for two drivers who were both gifted and who each had an unquenchable desire to always cross the finish line first. Friction on and off the track drove them apart professionally and personally. Their high-speed battles became legendary.

Senna did, however, have many friends among the other drivers. He was willing to leave the competition at the track and focus on friendship after hours.

On that day in Adelaide, the race was over, the season was over, and Alain Prost's career was at an end. In every way, it was "after hours." Prost, observing protocol, extended a hand to Ayrton for a reserved but proper handshake. Senna, in turn, grabbed Alain's hand firmly and pulled him up to stand beside him on the top podium. Then, with his arm securely around Alain's shoulders, he motioned the driver on the third place podium to step up and join them.

Considering past history, Alain Prost was, no doubt, a bit confused by the tribute and gesture of affection. But it was totally sincere, totally Senna.

Watching that replay of Senna's fellowshipping skills almost a year-and-a-half after it actually happened, I was startled to hear a voice within me whisper, "Learn to go and do likewise."

Clearly, for me, eliminating walls was not enough. I needed to be able to reach out to others, even reach over other walls when possible.

That March twenty-first whisper propelled me to make a comprehensive review of Ayrton Senna's brief but influential thirty-four years. Looking back, via books and videos, I couldn't help but make some comparisons between his outlook and my own "pre-magic-day" view of things. Although access to the restored gospel had given me insight into some true principles, which he had not yet discovered, I was only beginning to understand the unconditional love that characterized his relationships and that he demonstrated so naturally. He was a remarkable resource, a great example. He had sunshine enough and to spare. He once said, "Many plans have been in my mind for a long time, but I haven't found a way to put them into action . . . And all these plans come from a dream . . . I see other people happy because of them."

Ayrton may have thought the realization of his dream was still future, but during his lifetime he spread so much joy.

In his absence, his family has found a way to put his plans into action. Through the Ayrton Senna Foundation and Institute, they have channeled his formidable financial resources into charitable causes for the symbols "of life, of family, of the present, and of the future"—into nutrition, education, and inspiration for the children.

In this, his dream of making people happy continues to come true.

Each of us, in unique ways, can spread the sunshine of personal worth and ease the burdens of others. We can give them a hug and a handshake. We can "fly a flag" for them. We can give them a belief in themselves and the hope of victory. We can make their pathway bright, fill their souls with heaven's light. We can tell them that they are royalty!

And whenever we look in a mirror, we can remind ourselves of that glorious heritage. Then, even if the reflection we see has protruding eyes and seems to croak, we can blow a kiss, turn that frog into a prince or princess and, very quickly, straighten that crown!

TRUE HEROES

You can do a kindly deed
To your neighbor in his need,
If there's sunshine in your heart;
And his burden you will share
As you lift his load of care,
If there's sunshine in your heart today.
(*Hymns*, no. 228)

The good Samaritan of the Savior's famous parable did an exemplary kindly deed and thereby became a timeless hero.

A man traveling from Jerusalem to Jericho had been beaten and robbed. A priest and a Levite, pious citizens of the nation of Judah, afterward traveled the same road but, seeing the wounded man, passed by on the other side. Then one of the despised nation of Samaria happened by, "and when he saw him, he had compassion on him." The Samaritan bound up the man's wounds, took him to an inn, and paid his bills. He was a neighbor to him who fell among thieves (see Luke 10:29–37).

Along with compassion, the good Samaritan possessed sunshine and spontaneity. The Savior concluded the lesson of that parable with the directive: "Go, and do thou like-wise."

To be a good neighbor is to recognize the infinite worth of every soul, to promote humanity, to "defend the poor and fatherless: do justice to the afflicted and needy" (Psalm 82:3); to "succor the weak, lift up the hands which hang down, and strengthen the feeble knees" (D&C 81:5); and to understand that we are all beggars and that we all depend upon God for the substance which we have (see Mosiah 4:19). To be a good neighbor is to do as the good Samaritan did: use the resources our Father in Heaven has given us to bless the lives of His other children.

Speaking of our neighborly duties, President Howard W. Hunter taught that God "will measure our devotion to him by how we love and serve our fellowmen." Then he ques-tioned, "Does the test show us to be 24-karat gold, or can the trace of fool's gold be detected?" (*Ensign*, Nov. 1986, 34).

"Fool's gold service" is service done for reasons other than love, while "24-karat gold" people give sincere gifts from their hearts. They are true heroes and have sunshine to give away.

Of the many tributes paid Ayrton Senna, this one best summarized the feelings of his countrymen for him: "There are flesh and blood heroes, yes, and they are the best because they are closest to us. They represent our anxieties, our hopes, our aspirations, and they have a gift that only true heroes have: they never die even if they die and are buried, because they live in our memories, . . . I think . . . we must keep alive those memories, maintain access to our heroes.

There are not many of these heroes, and we protect them like the rarest of roses. They are few, Ayrton, and you are the most loved of all" (Raul Drewnick, "Faz um ano, Ayrton, e não nos esqueçemos,"—"A year has passed, Ayrton, and we haven't forgotten," *Estado de São Paulo*, May 2, 1995, C2).

Ayrton Senna gave much in donations of time and money, a substantial portion contributed quietly, even anonymously, and never known publicly until after his death; but news of his generosity was not surprising. People already believed he had a heart of gold.

In Portuguese, the word for compassionate service is *solidariedade*, or solidarity. Perhaps because it is a political word in some circles, I didn't understand it well until that day in May. Then I saw solidarity: people united in tribute, in love, in service. On that day, Brazil was "one." The gospel was being put in action, for the people demonstrated their willingness "to bear one another's burdens, that they may be light; Yea, and . . . willing to mourn with those that mourn; yea, and comfort those that stand in need of comfort" (Mosiah 18:8–9).

A little more *solidariedade* demonstrated everyday, everywhere, would bless the world with comfort and joy.

Consider the example of one woman. Ada was vibrant and young. She loved cats and people and life. She was a flight attendant for American Airlines, and she was terminally ill, but her illness did not snuff out her sunshine. One of the last gifts of her heart was to establish a compassionate service organization at American Airlines called

"Wings" to provide comfort and aid to current and former employees.

Shortly after her death, her husband gave us a letter from her, which she had written several weeks earlier. The letter itself was a gift from her heart, and in it she talked about sunshine.

"Since our death rarely allows us the luxury of closing with each of our loved ones . . . I am providing one in this way. I want to share some things that I've learned in the past several years that I feel everyone could benefit from. . . . After being told that my cancer was back a third time, I looked into heaven and said, 'Okay, God, you got my attention . . .—Now what? I'm only one, still I'm one. I cannot do everything but still I can do something and I will not refuse to do this something.' You know, God heard me that day because he kept me busy from that day forward. I've never been happier or felt more fulfilled. He did this for me in the form of my beloved 'Wings'. . . .

"There are so many stories I could share with you today but one immediately comes to mind (of) one Easter morning before I was out of bed. My husband handed me the phone, and in very broken deliberate words this dear flight attendant . . . said to me, 'Thank you for my Easter basket, I love it and I love you,' and hung up. I burst into tears of joy knowing that we as a group at 'Wings' could make such an impact on her life. I realized that we were not put there for her, she was put there for us.

"You don't get to choose how you're going to die or when; you can only decide how you're going to live now. In life it doesn't matter what happens around us or what happens to us. The final important thing is what happens in us.

"My life was full and happy due to all of you who touched it in so many ways. Please don't think of me with sadness. . . . Rather, think of me with joy." (A Personal Memorial Message by Ada Asher, used by permission of Keith Asher).

Ada made lemonade for herself and others by encouraging *solidariedade*. In giving, she found joy. "Wings" lifts burdens and goes on without her. Perhaps she will be remembered over time, perhaps not. Since the gift was from her heart, recognition was never her goal.

People who serve sincerely don't do it for recognition, although that may be a by-product. For example, historically: Florence Nightingale and George Washington; scripturally, Ruth and Naomi. In what they accomplished, they were just meeting the needs of people around them.

Elder Neal A. Maxwell has suggested: "We . . . should carry jumper and tow cables not only in our cars, but also in our hearts, by which means we can send the needed boost or charge of encouragement or the added momentum to [our] neighbors" (*All These Things Shall Give Thee Experience* [1980], 56).

Jumper cables connected in our hearts send little sparks of sunshine. People who carry such equipment choose to stop and help instead of passing by.

My husband and I had been living in Mexico City just five weeks and were spending a Saturday afternoon exploring the hills and dales of our new home. Late in the afternoon, we headed west to the national park and convent at *Desierto de Los Leones*.

As we passed through the last residential section before entering the park, we saw a white sedan barreling at a high rate of speed down the road toward us. We slowed and pulled close to a concrete embankment on the right. The driver of the sedan zigged to the right to miss a pothole and then to the left to avoid hitting a truck. Then he lost control.

As he slammed into our left front fender, metal crunched, the windshield cracked, and the left windows splattered into the backseat. The right rear of our car buckled against the concrete and the sedan slid down the left side, shearing off the metal and exposing a heavy interior bar of the door, which had saved our lives.

The fender of the sedan was crumpled around its left front tire, inhibiting further movement. The driver made a quick exit and disappeared, running across a field.

Behind us, the occupants of a white Volkswagon Beetle watched in horror, believing they were about to witness a fatal accident. They were also foreigners, from England and Italy, and were the first to provide us help and comfort.

"Are you hurt?"

"No, not badly."

"We saw it all," they continued. "We'll stay to help and to testify."

And stay they did, from 4:00 P.M. when the accident occurred until almost 9:00 P.M. when most of the Mexican red tape had been untangled.

We appreciated them. They were under no obligation to help, but, in spite of the inconvenience to themselves, they were willing.

We took them to dinner the next month, and we talked about how lucky we had all been that day. We had a protective bar in our favor, and they had us. If they had absorbed the impact instead of us, we never would have met. The careening sedan would have surely killed them both.

Though we have lost touch with our friends of the *Desierto* accident, we fondly remember them. One dinner seems hardly enough to repay them for their concern and the long hours they voluntarily kept us company by the roadside.

In so many life-trials and life-joys, we need one another. The ways to serve others are as numerous as the people with needs and those available to fill those needs: to wait with those who need to wait; to celebrate with those who have cause to celebrate; to mourn with those that mourn; to share words or cookies with anyone—anytime; to run with someone who wants to run; to sit with someone who wants to sit; to listen to someone who needs to talk; to talk to someone who needs advice; to correct someone who needs correction—and to know which to do, when; to hug a friend—or an enemy; to "fly a flag" for someone needing love and encouragement. There is joy in every kind of service, and big service projects are no more valid than daily acts of kindness. It is also true that service done abroad in the world is no more important than that offered sincerely within the walls of our own homes.

"There are so many times when genuine human service means giving graciously our little grain of sand, placing it reverently to build the beach of brotherhood. We get no receipt, and our little grain of sand carries no brand; its identity is lost, except to the Lord" (Neal A. Maxwell, *All These Things Shall Give Thee Experience* [1980], 63).

As a newly married military couple, our meager paycheck often didn't quite reach to the end of the month. Usually we could scrimp by, but one month funds were exhausted with an entire week left to go. We were pondering a plan of action on a Sunday evening when my husband checked the pockets of his well-worn suit coat, a relic from his missionary days. To our amazement and emotional relief, he encountered an unexpected treasure: a five-dollar bill— in those days enough to get us through.

Was it misplaced? An oversight on our part? It's doubtful. We had counted every penny. The only plausible explanation was that it had been placed there by an anonymous good Samaritan.

Such a little thing—five dollars; but to us it was a 24-karat gold fortune.

Years later, while we were on an international assignment in Johannesburg, the African girl who cleaned the floors in our block of apartments came to me with tear-filled eyes. Because I didn't often need her services, she didn't know me well. Hesitantly, she asked if I could give her a Rand (about $1.50) so she could take the bus to visit her critically ill sister in the hospital. She had asked others without success. She had no way to make repayment.

I pressed the Rand plus some change into her hand and sent her on her way.

The next day, upon returning home from a meeting, I found my kitchen sparkling clean with all the dirty dishes washed and dried.

One Rand. Such a little thing, I thought; but then I remembered the five dollars, and I knew that, to her, one Rand plus change was a 24-karat gold fortune.

Whether acts of service are large or small, one of the certainties is that calls to serve rarely come when we are waiting for them. Plans, meals, work, even sleep are often interrupted by requests for assistance; but these unexpected cries for help should not be resented. Since we can never predict when someone else's needs will cross our path, we must cultivate perpetual spontaneity.

"There was a little crippled boy who ran a small news-stand in a crowded railroad station. He must have been about twelve years old. Every day he would sell papers, candy, gum, and magazines to the thousands of commuters passing through the terminal.

"One night two men were rushing through the crowded station to catch a train. One was fifteen or twenty yards in front of the other. It was Christmas eve. Their train was scheduled to depart in a matter of minutes.

"The first man turned a corner and in his haste to get home to a Christmas cocktail party plowed right into the little crippled boy. He knocked him off his stool, and candy, newspapers, and gum were scattered everywhere. Without so much as stopping, he cursed the little fellow for being there and rushed on to catch the train that would take him to celebrate Christmas in the way he had chosen for himself.

"It was only a matter of seconds before the second commuter arrived on the scene. He stopped, knelt, and gently picked up the boy. After making sure the child was unhurt, the man gathered up the scattered newspapers, sweets, and magazines. Then he took his wallet and gave the boy a five-dollar bill. 'Son,' he said, 'I think this will take care of what was lost or soiled. Merry Christmas!'

"Without waiting for a reply, the commuter now picked up his briefcase and started to hurry away. As he did, the little crippled boy cupped his hands together and called out, 'Mister, Mister!'

"The man stopped as the boy asked, 'Are you Jesus Christ?'

"By the look on his face, it was obvious the commuter was embarrassed by the question. But he smiled and said, 'No, son. I am not Jesus Christ, but I am trying hard to do what He would do if He were here'" (Tom Anderson, *American Opinion*, December 1971, 13–14; quoted in Relief Society Course of Study, 1987, 134).

To do as Jesus would do if He were here, to follow His example, is the challenge, the goal of a lifetime: to give genuine, loving gifts from the heart.

True heroes, those who will be heroes "even if they die and are buried," have no stereotype. They might be rich and famous or of humble circumstances and virtually unknown; and *they* can be any one of *us*. True heroes have just one thing in common: they give 24-karat gold love and service. With joyful *solidariedade*, they scatter sparks of sunshine full of gifts from their hearts and, though they are seldom military leaders, they are the real victors of the battle—for sooner or later, love conquers all.

SILVER LININGS

"For it must needs be, that there is an opposition in all things" (2 Nephi 2:11).

Happiness will have its counterpart—sorrow and suffering. That is the nature of mortality, and, because it is, we often feel we have a right to grumble about life, at least in the hidden recesses of our minds. Though I have looked, I cannot find a gospel precedent for grumbling. In fact, the Lord has directed us: "In the world ye shall have tribulation: but be of good cheer" (John 16:33).

Elder Joe J. Christensen has elaborated: "The Lord does not say, 'Be of good cheer if the temperature is comfortable, if you're getting along well economically, if the people you love love you, if you're in good health, or if your "biorhythms" are up.' The Lord said that we should 'be of good cheer.' It is *not* a suggestion—it is a *commandment*" (*To Grow in Spirit* [1983], 34).

To be of good cheer on a regular basis, we must often turn the clouds of life inside out to reveal the silver linings. On that day in May, my Brazilian friends certainly made their cloud reversible:

"Life is eternal. We'll see you soon."

"We miss you, but there is joy in heaven."

With that kind of optimism, the silver linings glow and endings turn into beginnings:

"A conversation with the Lord: 'Lord! By chance has a young man driving a blue car at high speed arrived? It's our Ayrton, Lord, . . . If he's arrived, give him the checkered flag . . . because even though he doesn't know it, he won. Give him your hand, Lord, to help him out of the car. He could be a little surprised and lost because he left here at the speed of light . . . without time to say goodbye to the more than 150 million Brazilians—without counting all the other nationalities around the world. Whisper to him, Lord, so that he can envision the greatest expression of gratitude and love of a people that ever a mortal received. Convey to him, Lord, the most sincere gratitude for all these years of glory and struggle . . . '" (Photograph by Orípides Ribeiro of a poster at the Morumbi Cemetery, printed in *Revista Manchete*, May 6, 1995, 8).

I feel confident in saying that many Brazilians have already planned a reunion with their hero.

"Now the God of hope fill you with all joy and peace in believing" (Romans 15:13).

I went to college with a young woman who had cerebral palsy. Getting around campus was difficult for her, talking was tiring, writing was almost impossible. Yet she found ways to be where she needed to be, say what she needed to say, and successfully complete her schoolwork. Sitting in the lobby of the institute of religion one day, I overheard her haltingly and wistfully express her faith and hope: "One day, in the resurrection, I will be able to run, too."

Old Testament hero and inspiring example of endurance, Job, countered with his testimony when his neighbors taunted him and suggested that he curse God in response to his afflictions and losses: "I know that my redeemer liveth, and that he shall stand at the latter day upon the earth: And though after my skin worms destroy this body, yet in my flesh shall I see God" (Job 19:25–26).

Lasting joy is not a result of physical comfort or of always having things our way. Sometimes joy is just the certainty of light at the end of a long, dark tunnel and trust that our experiences will ultimately have value.

Incarcerated at Liberty, Missouri, in a cold and filthy cell, Joseph Smith was told to focus on the silver lining: "[I]f thou shouldst be cast into the pit, or into the hands of murderers, and the sentence of death passed upon thee; if thou be cast into the deep; if the billowing surge conspire against thee; if fierce winds become thine enemy; if the heavens gather blackness, and all the elements combine to hedge up the way; and above all, if the very jaws of hell shall gape open the mouth wide after thee, *know thou, my son, that all these things shall give thee experience, and shall be for thy good*" (D&C 122:7; emphasis added).

Joseph and the Saints of the Restoration were subjected to every type of indignity, persecution, and violent crime— acts so revolting that they were described as "dark and blackening deeds . . . enough to make hell itself shudder, and to stand aghast and pale, and the hands of the very devil to tremble and palsy" (D&C 123:10). Even in the face of such horror, the Church was directed: "Therefore, dearly beloved brethren, let us cheerfully do all things that lie in our power; and then may we stand still, with the utmost assurance, to see the salvation of God, and for his arm to be revealed" (D&C 123:17).

The Saints were to deal with the legal and emotional aspects of the circumstances and do so *cheerfully*. That sunshine word indicates that their response to the crimes committed against them was not to include hate or personal vengeance. They were not to let resentment obscure their vision and canker their souls. Rather, after doing all they could do as Christians, they were to wait upon God who would one day exact a perfect accountability from the perpetrators of evil.

In these latter days, with violence on the increase and more and more innocent lives being impacted by "dark and blackening deeds," the advice given to those in the early days of the Church who suffered at the hands of others still applies. Through application of that counsel, the wrenching trauma can be diffused. God can intervene. While leaving Nauvoo in an atmosphere of pain and infinite injustice, the pioneers were told: "If thou art sorrowful, call on the Lord thy God with supplication, that your souls may be joyful" (D&C 136:29).

The trials of mortality differ for each of us. Some are visible. Some are not. None is easy. All require effort to locate the sunshine.

Diane Ellingson, a champion gymnast paralyzed in a training accident, drifted into despair until a priesthood blessing revealed the silver lining. Later she wrote in her journal:

"I'm so afraid of having to live my whole life in the

prison of a body I can't move, on the seat of a wheelchair. At the same time, I know that I'll learn to conquer my fears. My Heavenly Father loves me and with my hand in his, I know he will be with me. My weakness will become my strength, and whether God allows me to walk again or not, I will accomplish his purpose and live a happy and fulfilling life" (Renon Klossner Hulet, *Don't You Dare Give Up* [1991], 180).

With such long-term tribulation as permanent paralysis, one batch of lemonade may not last. There may be a need to constantly mix new pitchers full. Actor Christopher Reeve—as famous for his courage facing life as a quadriplegic as for his movie role as Superman—emphasizes, in response to those who marvel at his optimism, "They don't know what I go through in the middle of the night" (*TIME International*, August 26, 1996, 41).

Sometimes the trial is within us—a need to overcome a personal weakness, challenge, or disability. Other times it is the burden of a wayward or suffering loved one when it seems our hands are tied and there is nothing we can do. If there really are no options, then we need to be willing to cast our burden at His feet, ask Him to take it from us, allow Him to intervene. "Cast thy burden upon the Lord, and he shall sustain thee" (Psalm 55:22).

The father of the prodigal son certainly had no recourse but prayer (see Luke 15:11–32). Alma the elder, after all the teaching he could do, left his son in the Lord's hands (see Mosiah 27:14). In these cases there were happy endings, but that is not always true. Each individual is free to choose happiness or misery, even after divine intervention. Lehi's sons Laman and Lemuel even rejected angels (see 1 Nephi 3:28–31; 4:3–4; 7:9-11). In the end, we cannot carry the weight of everyone's poor choices.

When we are despairing, not knowing what to do or where to turn, burdened with guilt or fear or pain, only One has the power to understand and respond. Jesus descended below all things in Gethsemane to save us in both time and eternity. "[H]e suffereth the pains of all men, yea, the pains of every living creature, both men, women, and children, who belong to the family of Adam" (2 Nephi 9:21).

No matter how lost and alone we feel, He has experienced even more physical, emotional, social, and spiritual suffering. With His help we can be healed and given peace, with or without final resolution of the problem. "Come unto me, all ye that labour and are heavy laden, and I will give you rest" (Matthew 11:28).

I was struggling with a proposed task, debating about the possibilities. I had faced the same challenge before with little success. After hours of analysis, none of the approaches I envisioned for the situation seemed feasible. I knew that given slightly different circumstances I could make a difference. I had the ability. I also knew that I could not control the variables of this particular situation. Some things would spin out of control in spite of all I could do. Was there no way to avoid the seemingly inevitable chaos? Every path I visualized ended in a state of confusion.

Feeling the storm-tossed sea within me stir up a desire to escape, my mind cried out, "I do not have the tools to deal with the variables. How should I proceed?" Then I felt a calm assurance: "I have the tools. Lean on me."

In seconds the stormy sea was quiet, and, though challenges lay ahead, I was at peace.

"God moves in a mysterious way" (*Hymns*, no. 285). Sometimes only after the fact do we understand the method.

While on his mission in Uruguay, my husband served in various capacities with members, ending his term of service by being a branch president over two new branches. Never, though, did he serve as a leader among his peers—not as a district leader, not as a zone leader, not as an assistant. Leaving the mission field, he wondered why. Was he unworthy of or incapable of handling those responsibilities? He had done his best in all he was asked to do, still the question remained.

Then, years later, he was called to be a bishop. After the sustaining and ordaining, as he settled into his office and the duties of the call, he realized he knew exactly what was expected of him. The Spirit then confirmed the long-awaited answer: "You received your leadership training through business opportunities. You received your ecclesiastical training on your mission."

Then he understood that God always knew what he needed.

The way He leads us is often not what we expect. God's ways are not man's ways. But we have His promise, "Be of good cheer, for I will lead you along" (D&C 78:18).

He will not interfere with our agency, and He does not

bring a halt to the winds, rains, tornadoes, and hurricanes of life; but He can give us the strength and wisdom to deal with those tempests. He is the rock on which we must build so that when the rains descend and the floods come and the winds blow and beat upon our house, it will not fall (see Matthew 7:24–25).

A friend of mine suggested: "None of us deserve a perfect set of circumstances. The only One who lived a perfect life was Jesus, and we certainly don't read of Him bemoaning His fate . . . He had anything but perfect circumstances to flourish under, so how can we possibly expect them for ourselves?"

Yet we can make the best of every situation and turn the night of any circumstance to day.

> When the days are gloomy,
> Sing some happy song;
> Meet the world's repining
> With a courage strong.
> Go with faith undaunted
> Through the ills of life;
> Scatter smiles and sunshine
> O'er its toil and strife.
> (*Hymns*, no. 230)

In the April 1996 general conference, Elder Henry B. Eyring of the Quorum of the Twelve Apostles spoke of his grandmother's sunshine attitude: "Grandmother Eyring learned from a doctor in his office that she would die of stomach cancer. My father, her oldest son, had driven her there and was waiting for her. He told me that on the way home she said, 'Now, Henry, let's be cheerful. Let's sing hymns.' They sang 'O My Father' (*Hymns*, no. 292) and 'Come, Come, Ye Saints,' where the last verse begins, 'And should we die before our journey's through . . . ' (*Hymns*, no. 30).

"I wasn't there, but I imagine they sang loudly—they didn't have very melodic voices—with faith and no tears" (*Ensign*, May 1996, 64). With or without tears, faith can give us the power to endure the pain, suffering, sorrow, and discouragement of life without despairing. Even when it seems there is nothing to applaud, with the Lord's help we can find the silver linings and the sunshine. We can go on with peace and vision and even joy.

"Hast thou not known? hast thou not heard, that the everlasting God, the Lord, the Creator of the ends of the earth, fainteth not, neither is weary? there is no searching of his understanding.

"He giveth power to the faint; and to them that have no might he increaseth strength. . . . [T]hey that wait upon the Lord shall renew their strength; they shall mount up with wings as eagles; they shall run, and not be weary; and they shall walk, and not faint" (Isaiah 40:28, 29, 31).

FINDING EQUILIBRIUM

LOVE. LEMONADE. SPONTANEITY. SUNSHINE. JOY!

Learning to sing the "sunshine serenade" was challenging but exhilarating. From hues of black and gray and other darker shades, my life became green, yellow, blue, and all the other colors of the rainbow. Perhaps the difference wasn't visible on the outside. I don't know. I don't often see the outside of me, but I know the transformation on the inside was absolutely night to day. The mighty change couldn't have been any more dramatic if someone had actually waved a magic wand and "abracadabra-ed" me into a new creature.

The lessons, the sunshine—the initial magic and the subsequent related enlightenment—were all a miraculous mellowing force. I felt as though I had lived my life up to that point slightly out of balance and suddenly had acquired equilibrium. Life was often tough, but it did not have to be such serious business.

I learned that the world didn't collapse if I sometimes said "no," and I seemed to have a pretty good sense of when "no" was the right answer. Persistent worry was abandoned since it didn't change any outcomes. I made reasonable personal progress even when I wasn't always so hard on myself, and others did pretty well when I wasn't so hard on them. It became easier to see when I should add frills to life and when I should simplify. I could usually tell when to speak up and when to shut up; when to communicate from the heart, impromptu, and when to pronounce each word, each sentence, with caution. I even drew a "line in the sand" and began practicing the art of controlling my space. When appropriate I would stand my ground and not allow myself to be manipulated.

With this equilibrium, discouragement and depression fled. I couldn't remember the last time I had carried a chip on my shoulder. Life didn't offend me anymore and neither did anyone in it, in spite of the imperfections in both. Arbitrary opinions no longer swayed me. Things I could not change no longer wore me down. I stopped wishing for the ideal, yet each day was worth celebrating. With so many walls gone, I felt liberated.

Those barriers, in a word, were a tendency to be critical—of life, people in it, and myself. Before that magic day, few things were ever acceptable because they were not the way I wanted them to be and did not behave in the way I wanted them to. I viewed life as unruly, people as offensive, and I was never at peace with who and where I was personally. I consistently accentuated the negatives and ignored the positives.

While these attitudes generally lived out of sight in my mind and heart and seldom translated to behavior that others could see, they were very effective at keeping resentment and pessimism stirred up in me. Just because they were invisible did not minimize their power to suppress peace and joy.

When my mind was so miraculously opened to all the positives in Brazil, all that the people there could teach me, a kind of domino effect occurred as I began to see affirmative aspects of everything. Eliminating more walls and adding on the other lessons gave me a new, exciting buoyancy. For months I emotionally and mentally somersaulted and "samba-ed" through life, soaring high, seeing nothing but sunshine everywhere.

I guess it was inevitable that I would eventually "fall back to earth." Suddenly I found myself in a whirlpool where my time was not my own, my responsibilities were less than enjoyable, I was not getting proper sleep, food, or exercise, and my associates were driving me berserk. As a result, the light dimmed, a wall popped up, and I justified it by saying life was tough.

"It's okay," I said to myself. "I'm sure I'm allowed to commiserate once in a while. I know how to get rid of the wall eventually."

But I forgot that the longer one of those walls is in place, the higher it grows and the harder it is to destroy. Fortunately for me I rediscovered the "true grit" formula, so this new wall didn't rise above ground floor.

One day, as I was cleaning the clutter off my desk, I uncovered a scrap of paper on which I had written the rule. When I read it, my hard heart quickly melted.

"When you're not happy, you need to be strong to change."

Brazil, in the person of Ayrton Senna, had come to my rescue. I was going to have to take charge of the situation in order to fly high once more.

I looked back at the "lemonade" recipe.

1. Think of good "stuff" and rejoice in it.
2. Don't hold back genuine, positive emotions.
3. Add a dash of spontaneity.
4. Focus on the present moment and make memories by seasoning with hope, gratitude, and love.

Good "stuff" hadn't been easy to find, so I stopped looking. All my emotions were of the negative variety. I had abandoned spontaneity. The only hope in evidence was a kind of resignation to survive the situation, and gratitude and love were hibernating.

The time had come to find the silver lining.

So far as the responsibilities were concerned, I was being stretched far out of my comfort zone—but that was good, not bad, although it was difficult. We can be stretched by choice or by circumstance, and I would have chosen to stretch in a different direction. Nevertheless, I would have to take the detour and enjoy the journey.

With regard to my attitude toward my associates, it occurred to me that "Fools mock . . ." and that I was being the fool. I was refusing to accept them as they were, demanding that they conform to my expectations, requiring that they meet me on my turf when, instead, I should have been willing to try and meet them on theirs—or at least go halfway. All I needed to do was see the good in them and then force myself out of my comfort zone. More than a little "true grit" would be needed, but I was sure I could practice and learn, little by little.

I was beginning to understand that with a sunshine attitude, it is possible to stretch farther than we ever have before to learn, improve, achieve our goals, and serve others. I also realized that, operating with the light, we are able to prioritize our time even though some days have only the briefest moments available. I found that maintaining a sunshine attitude requires reserving some of my time—for me—for use in cultivating my own spiritual and physical well-being and doing the things I really love.

With sunshine you will want to pen a poem, paint a picture, play the piano, take guitar lessons, redecorate a room, plant a garden, knit a sweater, keep a journal, take a college class, compose a song, design a tree house, have a dinner party, decorate a birthday cake, make a rag doll, build a boat, invent the ultimate something-or-other.

If you love music, turn on the stereo; buy opera tickets.

If you love fishing, locate the nearest pond.

If you feel liberated by reading and writing, stake out a rocking chair and a computer.

If you love the smell of the grease paint and revel in the roar of the crowd, join the nearest drama club.

Do it because you deserve it, and because there's nothing so exhilarating as spending a few minutes or a few hours doing your very own sunshine things.

But that coin has a flip side. My husband (one of the "eccentrics") enjoyed a story he heard about a great composer who was peeling an orange while being interviewed by newspaper reporters. One of the questioners, attempting to elicit some profound philosophy from the maestro, queried, "What is the most important thing you have ever done?" to which the musician quietly replied, "I am doing the most important thing I have ever done—peeling this orange."

I'll be honest. Back in my "before joy" stage, I didn't get it. Now I do! This particular moment in time, right now, this very minute, is the most valuable moment in time; and whatever we are doing (as long as it's not aiding and abetting the enemy) is important and deserves to be respected, even sometimes celebrated.

Sure, we'll occasionally choose to spend that moment doing a secondary thing instead of a primary thing: reading a book when we should be cooking dinner, enjoying computer games when we should be composing tomorrow's financial report, playing with the kids when we should be cleaning and weeding, or cleaning and weeding when we should be playing with the kids. We are only mortal, so we need to learn how to improve our ability to choose; but when we enjoy peeling the orange, even if we should be bobbing for apples, we will treasure the past and joyfully anticipate the future while still embracing the present. Any guilt about what we did or didn't do simply won't last very long. We need to plan less and live more, be flexible, respond with gusto to each circumstance instead of always checking the agenda, the "to do" list, or social expectations.

While social expectations are often of questionable value, "to do" lists and agendas do keep us from riding off in four directions at once; but so often we only pencil in sunshine-time, instead of writing it boldly in permanent ink. By irrevocably scheduling it, we can make sure it happens. There is an old Chinese proverb that says: "Man who sit with open mouth waiting for roast duck to fly in have long hunger." So it is with sunshine. We need to make it happen.

At the same time, unplanned, unscheduled, too often unrecognized magic moments are always zipping around. We just need to internalize them by putting on some rose-colored glasses.

Equilibrium is the magic ingredient in pacing ourselves so that we can act in wisdom and order and not run faster than we have strength (see Mosiah 4:27). We'll understand that we can be diligent daily without feeling eternally exhausted. We will balance relaxation with stretching and steady improvement. We will rejoice in baby steps, dream a little instead of just make plans, and respond smoothly to life's transitions. We will be too busy enjoying each day to stop and take measurements of how far we've come and how far we have yet to go. Instead, we'll just check our course headings: "Am I still on the straight and narrow path, learning life skills and gospel principles, and little by little improving?"

With practice and patience, we will learn to act for ourselves and not let ourselves be acted upon, not allow ourselves to be constantly blown about and tossed. We will be rooted and grounded in faith and hope. As we learn when to hold on and when to let go, we will cast our burdens at His feet. We will trust in His love. We will make lemonade. We will choose joy.

The "true grit" formula now hangs safely above the clutter on my desk. It reminds me that, even when life is tough, with determination and tenacity I can always find the light and go flying again. "Happy is the man that findeth wisdom, and the man that getteth understanding" (Proverbs 3:13).

Wisdom and understanding: synonyms, it seems to me, for equilibrium. Happy: just another word for sunshine.

WALKING IN
THE LIGHT

During all the years I walked in shadows, I believed I was only being realistic; but the realities of today's world instill pessimism unless we know how to exert personal power and "rise above the blues" (Mormonad, Series B), unless we have the keys to joy and light.

As I stood in the shadows in my "before-joy" frame of mind, I saw joy as a result—the pot of gold at the end of the rainbow—when, in reality, it should have been on-going and ever-present. It exists in various forms and various feelings. Because of its complexity, *joy* is not an easy word to define.

In the Topical Guide, there are numerous synonyms given for *joy:* cheerfulness, delight, gladness, happiness, pleasure. I have occasionally participated in discussions where attempts have been made to separate pleasure (daily fun), happiness (earthly goodness), and joy (eternal rewards); but that analysis suggests that pleasure has no value and makes joy something to be found only in the future. The scriptures mention something called a "fulness of joy," which is associated with immortality (D&C 93:33) and therefore will not be ours on earth, but "men are, that they might have joy" (2 Nephi 2:25) is present tense. The "are" is here and now and the "might have" focuses on our approach to the here and now—on our desires, decisions, and determination.

Though a fulness of joy is not yet ours, possession of a not quite full-blown joy can be ours in the present. In fact, when truly beautiful things happen to us, we marvel that greater feelings of euphoria might ever be ours. Eternal life, however, is more and better of everything.

Joy has a spectrum of intensity, and, while that eternal fullness will be the most vivid kind of joy, there are many present experiences that produce their own joyful colors.

There are pleasurable experiences such as taking roller coaster rides with a friend or even alone; eating cotton candy, double dipped ice cream cones, or Thanksgiving dinner; or buying a new car. These pleasurable temporal adventures set free a few chemicals in the brain called endorphins, which hop around and give us a sense of elation. Such a state doesn't last very long, but for a while we think we know what happiness is.

Feeling peace and contentment is another manifestation of joy. Because we live in a stressful world, we sometimes think of contentment and satisfaction as signs of laziness; and because we sometimes only see a gospel of endless effort, we interpret peace as an inappropriate state of being. The evening news and the scriptures are filled with stories charged with challenge and conflict. There are few examples of joyful contentment. There is no drama in the warmth of a fireplace, an easy chair, a good book, and a picture window. Nevertheless, such moments of peace are some of the highlights of our lives. We should relish them, soak them up, never let them simply slip away.

Significant events contribute to our joy—such things as weddings, parades, and an almost perfect Christmas day; graduations, family reunions, and even time spent lending a shoulder to cry on. Little things and big things that really mean a lot can trigger an eruption of joy.

There is also the thrill, the exhilaration, that comes from overcoming opposition, beating the odds, being stretched to the limit and surviving, maybe even winning.

We can also find joy in the rapture of learning a truth, finding a talent, or experiencing a mighty change of heart.

Joy is cheer and rejoicing and gladness and merry hearts, and these are all "good like a medicine" (Proverbs 17:22). There can be joy everywhere we turn in life: in temporal experiences, in social events, in spiritual awakenings, even in trials. Adam's life was not without its challenges, yet he declared, "in this life I shall have joy" (Moses 5:10). For him, joy was accessible, not something only to be wished for. Most of all, the joy that lifts us and lasts forever, the joy emphasized in the scriptures, is the joy of the gospel. Elder Richard G. Scott explains: "Your joy in life depends upon your trust in Heavenly Father and His holy Son, your conviction that their plan of happiness truly can bring you joy. Pondering their doctrine will let you enjoy the beauties of this earth and enrich your relationships with others. It will lead you to the comforting, strengthening experiences that flow from prayer to Father in Heaven and the answers He gives in return" (*Ensign*, May 1996, 24).

The key to finding joy is seizing the moment. Prior to absorbing the magic of that one Brazilian day, I was guilty of letting superfluous concerns distract me from the joy that might be available in any given situation. Many of us, even those of us who have the gospel in our lives, let joy slip through our fingers, by "looking beyond the mark" (Jacob 4:14).

My former tendency, to plod resolutely through life, focusing solemnly on weighty matters, was due in part to my misinterpretation of a scripture that says, "Cast away your idle thoughts and your excess of laughter far from you" (D&C 88:69). When I finally understood joy, I realized that when the Lord directs us to cast away our idle thoughts, he doesn't mean we can't enjoy satisfying moments of peace and contentment. And when I consulted the footnote to that verse, I learned that "excess of laughter" refers to rioting and reveling. There is a difference between the joyful peal of merriment (which is legitimate) and the boisterous din that comes of vulgarity and drunkenness or even irreverence. In life there are many behaviors and attitudes that appear to be desirable on the surface, that may even counterfeit joyful feelings temporarily, but which in the end leave cold despair instead of warm memories. The gospel teaches us how to separate the true from the false.

That we *might* have joy suggests there is a possibility of

joy. There is no guarantee, but the ball is in our court. We will find joy, if we seek joy.

I was once bound to a long-term Church assignment that was extremely difficult for me and, therefore, I queried, "Is it enough for me to fulfill this calling willingly or do I have to do it cheerfully, too?" At the time I concluded that *willingly* would have to fly solo. I endured it, but I'm now convinced I did not endure it well (see D&C 121:8). To endure well is to "live a happy life In this world of toil and strife" (*Hymns*, no. 228). Being happy is an outward manifestation of the "sunshine in your heart."

Joy and *cheer* and *merry hearts* are not the only sunshine words. *Faith, hope, gratitude, love*, and many other joyful things are also conveyors of light; and, when one of them comes through the door with real intent, somehow the others follow, all holding hands.

Perhaps we have so much difficulty dealing with sunshine these days because joy is an emotion, a feeling, and we do not know exactly what to do with emotions and feelings. The age of technology is an age of logic and reason; and, though we do need logic to be focused and consistent and efficient, emotions are a very real and important part of our being. Too often, however, we repress rather than express them, or we allow our expression to be dictated by the expectations of society. To get bubbly over a new car in our materialistic society is okay, but getting bubbly over the gospel is viewed as weird. Ammon, however, was absolutely effervescent in his description of his joy in the gospel: "Blessed be the name of our God; let us sing to his praise, yea, let us give thanks to his holy name, for he doth work righteousness forever. . . . Behold, my joy is full, yea, my heart is brim with joy, and I will rejoice in my God. . . .

"Now have we not reason to rejoice? Yea, I say unto you, there never were men that had so great reason to rejoice as we, since the world began; yea, and my joy is carried away, even unto boasting in my God. . . . Now if this is boasting, even so will I boast; for this is my life and my light, my joy and my salvation" (Alma 26:8, 11, 35, 36).

Most of our scriptural indicators for joy come from the Book of Mormon. Apparently the Nephites understood the doctrine of joy and were comfortable with it. Perhaps this is so because they were comfortable expressing their emotions, as evidenced in Ammon's impassioned testimony, Lamoni's dramatic conversion, Nephi's psalm, the people's unbridled emotional response to the Savior's visit, and both Mormon's and Moroni's lamentations for their people (See Alma 26; Alma 18–19; 2 Nephi 4:15–35; 3 Nephi 11-28; Mormon 6–8). Expressed emotions seem to have been a building block of their lifestyle.

The scriptural corollary for emotions and feelings is the word *heart*, as differentiated from *mind*. The Lord directed those who embark in his service to "see that ye serve him with all your heart, might, mind and strength" (D&C 4:2).

In other places, the scriptures say:

" . . . let thy heart cheer thee . . ." (Ecclesiastes 11:9).

" . . . love one another with a pure heart . . ." (1 Peter 1:22).

" . . . why should my heart weep . . ." (2 Nephi 4:26).

" . . . I will tell you in your mind and in your heart . . ." (D&C 8:2).

There is in our hymnal the wonderful assurance that we can set aside the discouraging things in our life and have our burdens lifted if we but have "sunshine in [our] heart[s]" (*Hymns*, no. 228).

When conversion takes place, the emotions are involved, and those who are touched by the Spirit are said to experience "a mighty change [of heart]" (see Mosiah 5:2; Alma 5:14). Among the sacrifices that are acceptable to God are "a broken and contrite heart" (Psalm 51:17; see also D&C 56:18). Where there is humility, repentance, and a desire to improve, there is also emotion. Nevertheless, a demonstration of emotion is not always a sign of testimony, for our emotions can betray and mislead us. See, for instance, these statements: "[T]he power of Satan . . . did get hold upon their hearts" (4 Nephi 1:28); "[T]hou shalt not be proud in thy heart" (D&C 42:40); "[T]heir hearts are set so much upon the things of this world . . ." (D&C 121:35).

Just because our emotions make us vulnerable, however, does not mean we should try to eliminate them. The things we are capable of *feeling* help put us in touch with the things of the Spirit. But we do have a duty to bridle our emotions and to make proper use of them. Consider these insights from the scriptures: "For I, the Lord, will judge all men according to their works, according to the desire of their hearts" (D&C 137:9); "[C]ome unto the Lord with all your heart" (Mormon 9:27); "[L]ay up for yourselves treasures in heaven . . . for where your treasure is, there will your heart be also" (Matthew 6:20–21).

Emotions must be controlled. For example, we must learn to be patient and long-suffering, to restrain anger and choose right from wrong; but there is also a time when it is legitimate to express grief and sorrow as well as a time to enjoy excitement, to celebrate, and to be joyful.

Finding equilibrium in this emotional melting pot isn't easy. Occasionally, we'll feel like inept jugglers. In acquiring patience and other important character traits, we often feel frustrated as we try and try again. Because of cultural mores, we are sometimes embarrassed by our response to tenderness and sentiment and to grief and sorrow, forgetting the moments when even "Jesus wept" (John 11:35; see also 3 Nephi 17:21). And in our stressed society we seldom spend enough time rejoicing—doing mental cartwheels and enthusiastically throwing handfuls of confetti. We need more boundless optimism and exuberant celebration.

To handle each emotion properly and appropriately, requires practice and dexterity. To mix all the feelings together and brew a palatable experience from the potpourri demands a bit of magic, and what I admired in my Brazilian friends was their ability to give appropriate expression to their emotions. On that magic day in May, they balanced a multitude of emotions to near perfection. Awed by their "gift," I went in search of the principles and found the light. "[S]eek, and ye shall find" (Matthew 7:7; Luke 11:9) is as valid where joy is concerned as it is with any other gospel doctrine. Once I discovered the truth, the real work of practicing and applying those principles began. Fortunately, I also learned that I was strong enough to change.

In time, it became more and more automatic for me to turn the lemons life hands me into lemonade. With my willingness to do so came a receptivity to additional truths. Resentment and murmuring rarely surfaced, and, when they did, I knew how to do battle and win. I found joy blossoming everywhere—in the scriptures, in the hymnbook, in the morning, in the evening, in the kitchen, and at the office. My testimony was stronger and brighter. Light was inside and out. I was able to follow the admonition of Paul, "[L]et us therefore cast off the works of darkness, and let us put on the armour of light" (Romans 13:12).

In the scriptures, *light* usually refers to truth, to obedience, to Jesus, to the Light of Christ, to life, to enlightenment, to testimony. "For the word of the Lord is truth, and whatsoever is truth is light, and whatsoever is light is Spirit, even the Spirit of Jesus Christ. And the Spirit giveth light to every man that cometh into the world; and the Spirit enlighteneth every man through the world, that hearkeneth to the voice of the Spirit. And every one that hearkeneth to the voice of the Spirit cometh unto God, even the Father" (D&C 84:45–47).

With a little sunshine in my heart, I felt that joy, in all its splendor, must also be included in the definition of light. Sometimes in reading, I would even substitute one word for the other:

"[M]en are, that they might have joy [light]" (2 Nephi 2:25).

"[I]n this life I shall have joy [light]" (Moses 5:10).

"He is the light [joy] and the life of the world" (Mosiah 16:9).

"Ye are all the children of light [joy]" (1 Thessalonians 5:5).

And even "God is light [joy], and in him is no darkness at all" (1 John 1:5). No darkness at all. Not even a drop.

Evil, on the other hand, loves darkness rather than light (joy). That great unhappy camper who has no light, no joy, and who desires only to make us as miserable as he is (see 2 Nephi 2:27), pulls and pushes us into the shadows. He distracts us with foreboding black clouds of despair while he plunges in daggers of discouragement. Then he keeps twisting the knife. He is a wholesale distributor of blindfolds and earplugs, which, if we accept his wares, leave us with neither ears to hear the music and laughter nor eyes to see the sunshine. Then the dark one dances in delight at our dejection.

I think that on that magic day in May, having been blinded by the light, he temporarily fled Brazil.

Our world, steeped in skepticism and false doctrine, seems to become more and more pessimistic every day. As a result, many look for happiness in temporal pleasures; but even pleasure of the best kind is such a thin, fragile beam of light that it dissipates almost before it can be captured. When it is gone, Satan still works his schemes. He NEVER gives up. Therefore, we must keep burning the eternal flame of faith, hope, gratitude, and love. We must believe in our worth, the value of life, and the power of gospel principles to make everything meaningful. These are the tools that give us the power to command, "Get thee hence, Satan" (Matthew 4:10).

There will be no darkness in us when we put on the "armour of light," when we have sunshine in our hearts, when we make Jesus and His gospel the source of our song.

Though Brazil has its share of social and moral problems —perhaps more than its share—there is nevertheless an abundance of faith in Jesus Christ among its citizens. With that foundation, many Brazilians eagerly listen to and accept the message of the missionaries. Then, possessing that increase of truth, their light glows even brighter.

I believe it is an irrefutable truth that *we* determine the amount of sunshine in our hearts, the amount of sunshine in each day, through the truths we embrace and the effort we exert to let our light shine.

I am a witness that it is never too late to embrace the joyful pathway, never too late to learn to walk in the light. "And that which doth not edify is not of God, and is darkness. That which is of God is light; and he that receiveth light, and continueth in God, receiveth more light; and that light groweth brighter and brighter until the perfect day. And again, verily I say unto you, and I say it that you may know the truth, that you may chase darkness from among you" (D&C 50:23–25).

THANKS-GIVING

Over and over again, I found myself standing at the window of our nineteenth-floor apartment—on a hill, ten miles from the city center—looking out over São Paulo, soaking up the vista, memorizing the moods. After living almost fifteen years in Brazil, we were preparing to leave. Once upon a time I had looked forward to departure day but, of course, that was before I was touched with magic. More than three years had passed since the death of Ayrton Senna, but for me, São Paulo still felt magical—a place full of memories and miracles.

Framed in my nineteenth-floor window, the magnificence of São Paulo was breathtaking. I could see innumerable, thirty-story apartment buildings, some of them close enough to be in my neighborhood. Separated from each other by groves of trees and frozen in formation, the tall buildings stretched away to the left and to the right, as far as the eye could see—a never-ending line of soldiers, standing shoulder to shoulder. I remember thinking to myself that the sprawling city—with its density of population—must be one of the wonders of the modern world.

From my perch, ten miles away, the center of the city looked like a storybook land, a miniature of the real thing.

Overseeing it, I felt like a giant who could, at a whim, scoop up the tiny metropolis in the palm of my hand and bring it in to display on a shelf in the living room. Whenever I had been down there, in the middle of the traffic and cement and the hustle and bustle, I hadn't felt so powerful, so omnipotent; but from my window, I felt invincible and anything seemed possible.

Some days, when I was up before the sun, I watched the day dawn—the sky beginning to glow golden, the color creeping upward, slowly upward, turning into muted shades of pink streaked with silver and a hint of blue, the light silhouetting residential monoliths. There was renewal in watching that awe-inspiring birth of a new day.

Because my apartment faced the sunrise, I could not actually see the sun set from my window. But if I were watching at certain, precise moments at the end of the day, I was able to witness the sparkling reflection of the sunlight as it danced on the windows of the buildings down in the city—touching them briefly with a magic wand of fire and simultaneously illuminating the sky—before quickly fading into dusk. Those moments were sensational, staccato.

I also loved the nights, clear nights when the multi-million city lights twinkled and winked at me. I especially treasured the full-moon nights when that yellow-orange balloon would float tranquilly between those apartment towers to the east. In those moments I felt as though I could, with minimal effort, reach out and cradle the iridescent orb in my hands like a crystal ball and bring it inside to peruse up close for a moment.

During those São Paulo nights I often stood at the window, searching for more of the music to the "sunshine serenade." Sometimes harmonies drifted in on the breeze and I was free.

Clear nights always glistened, and the occasional foggy night covered the city like a shroud, hiding it from my view; but in daylight there were so many different faces.

There were stormy days when immense, threatening, black rain clouds hung over the city like a black umbrella, eerie and ominous, reminiscent of an enormous dark alien spacecraft in a major motion picture, which hovers over cities of the world waiting to rain down terror. Once in a while the black clouds over São Paulo unleashed their own kind of terror in the form of torrential downpours that brought the city and everyone unlucky enough to be down there in it to a standstill.

From my window only the wonder of it all, the splendid forces of nature—not the inconvenient, uncomfortable reality showed. Raindrops fell past my window on their way down. I often reached out to catch a refreshing handful.

On some days the distant skyline was obscured by haze, but generally I could distinguish the faint outline of those distant monoliths, the cement soldiers at attention in the fog. Once in a while the surreal science fiction feeling would return when the mist would settle thickly into the canyons between the buildings, leaving the skyscraper tops free to breathe. Then I would imagine São Paulo as the isolated capital city of some distant ethereal planet, where futuristic beings walked the concrete halls and spaceships soared into the universe from launch pads nestled among the obelisks in the swirling misty clouds. In that scenario, São Paulo seemed a forbidding place but, to me, never really foreign.

Though I loved all the faces of São Paulo, my favorite kind of day was when the sun smiled down from an unblemished azure sky and it seemed possible to see forever. It was on such a day that São Paulo and its people woke me up from a lifelong sleep and taught me the meaning of beauty and love.

As I watched the moods of the city during those last few days that I lived there, I knew that whenever I would think of São Paulo in the future I would envision it encompassed by an infinite heaven of brilliant blue filled with cascades of colorful rose petals and decorated with wispy valentines.

I knew how much I would miss my daily inspirational rendezvous with the city in the distance, but I knew how much farther I could see because of the lessons. Reminders of the magic filled me with awe and gratitude.

The phrase on a card sent by a friend summarized my adventure: "The real voyage of discovery consists not in seeking new landscapes but in having new eyes" (Marcel Proust).

My "new eyes" had given me a vivid appreciation for each day, and, in leaving São Paulo, they would go with me to make every future day beautiful. I had no walls to hinder my view, and in our new home in Santiago, Chile, I would not build any.

Because of my "new eyes," it was easy to be grateful. I found the "thank-you" part of my prayers growing longer, and I also learned fasting can be a joy when we do so to show our gratitude.

I thought of the many stories I had heard over the years about prisoners of war and concentration camp survivors who had held onto sunshine in the midst of misery; about the pilgrims who possessed so little yet managed a feast to give thanks; and of messages such as that found in 3 Nephi 10:10: "And the earth did cleave together again, that it stood; and the mourning, and the weeping, and the wailing of the people who were spared alive did cease; and their mourning was turned into joy, and their lamentations into praise and thanksgiving unto the Lord Jesus Christ, their Redeemer."

Truly, no matter how challenging life becomes, we need thanks-giving. "Verily I say unto you my friends, fear not, let your hearts be comforted; yea, rejoice evermore, and in everything give thanks" (D&C 98:1).

Preparing for departure caused me to look back carefully at the three years that had passed since the day my walls fell. During that time I had learned about personal power and lemonade, about careful and troubled people and their inability to be spontaneous or shout for joy, about self-worth and unconditional love, about heroes and service and silver linings. In the end I had found equilibrium and a pathway of light.

I often reflected on the fact that sometime before that day in May—feeling lost, alone, and discouraged, having tried unsuccessfully to change my attitudes—I had offered a prayer, a plea for help. I don't know what I expected in response. Certainly I did not expect magic.

Gratefully I acknowledge that it was the Spirit that instructed me to absorb the contrasting emotions of that day in May and that taught me how to harvest the sunshine.

Having found the light, I know I must now work to retain it. Alma's words about testimony apply: "[I]f you have felt to sing the song of redeeming love, I would ask, can ye feel so now?" (Alma 5:26).

I choose to feel the joy forever! I understand the truth of President Gordon B. Hinckley's counsel: "Life is to be enjoyed, not just endured" (*Ensign*, May 1996, 94).

Before departure, on a day when my personal sunshine felt particularly bright, it seemed appropriate for me to make a journey to a very green cemetery in São Paulo, to the final resting place of Brazil's hero.

There was no heart drawn in a bright blue sky that day. In fact, the clouds were gray, and a light drizzle was falling. I assumed the inclement weather would limit the procession of Senna's friends and fans from Brazil and around the world, who, even after the passage of so much time, continued to adorn his grave with flags and flowers; but I sat in the car for more than twenty minutes, watching groups, families, couples, and individuals arrive to pay their respects.

I waited patiently. I wanted to spend my moment alone.

Finally, as the drizzle intensified, everyone else departed. Taking a yellow bouquet in hand, I quickly climbed the slope to the prominent grave, situated under a flowering purple Ipé tree.

Except for the tap of raindrops on leaves, the cemetery was quiet. The ground-level grave markers created the appearance of a peaceful park of endless green, dotted here and there with flowers. Reverently, I laid my token offering of thanks next to the small bronze plaque on which were recorded Senna's name, the dates of his birth and death, and one short biblical phrase full of truth and sunshine:

"Nothing can separate me from the love of God" (see Romans 8:39).

Ayrton Senna was a seeker after truth, a giver of sun-shine, a man who lived a life worth celebrating, a life that had touched mine for good. I felt very much in his debt, very much like one of "his people."

On that rainy São Paulo day I reviewed all the sunshine lessons, ever-present in my life, ever-expanding. I will never forget. Would that I could give the players of that "one magic Brazilian day" my personal, sustained standing ovation.

Words came to mind, reminiscent of that day when it all began. Quietly I whispered them, with emotion straight from my heart.

"Thanks Ayrton and Brazil—for the JOY."

A few days later, while viewing the city scene from my São Paulo window, I made a list of mentors—people who had exerted positive influences in my life. So many of them I had never thanked and, because the majority were either in unknown locations or no longer in mortality, making a personal expression of gratitude was, for the moment, impossible. The future, however, could be different.

About that same time, I began to read Psalms in the Old Testament, something I had done only haphazardly before. In those poems, I found expressions of gratitude similar to the ones in my heart.

"When I consider thy heavens, the work of thy fingers, the moon and the stars, which thou hast ordained; What is man, that thou art mindful of him?" (Psalm 8:3–4). I was very aware of the individualized attention lavished on me while I was learning the sunshine lessons. It was obvious to me that, even though we don't understand how our Father in Heaven does it, He is very mindful of each one of His children.

"Sing aloud unto God our strength: make a joyful noise unto the God of Jacob. Take a psalm, and bring hither the timbrel, the pleasant harp with the psaltery. Blow up the trumpet in the new moon, in the time appointed, on our solemn feast day" (Psalm 81:1–3). In the music of that Psalm, I heard the "sunshine serenade."

"O give thanks unto the Lord; for he is good: for his mercy endureth for ever. O give thanks unto the God of gods: for his mercy endureth for ever. O give thanks to the Lord of lords: for his mercy endureth for ever" (Psalm 136:1–3). I had learned that His eternal mercy is the very foundation of the great plan of happiness.

In the much-loved twenty-third Psalm, I found beauty and peace as well as a particularly appropriate application:

THANKS-GIVING

The Lord is my shepherd; I shall not want.

He maketh me to lie down in green pastures: he leadeth me beside the still waters.

He restoreth my soul: he leadeth me in the paths of righteousness for his name's sake.

Yea, though I walk through the valley of the shadow of death, I will fear no evil: for thou art with me; thy rod and thy staff they comfort me.

Thou preparest a table before me in the presence of mine enemies: thou anointest my head with oil; my cup runneth over.

Surely goodness and mercy shall follow me all the days of my life: and I will dwell in the house of the Lord for ever.

The Psalms teach a sometimes-forgotten truth: there is nothing so effective as thanks-giving to make life wonderful and to ensure that, in all circumstances, "my cup runneth over." As Brazil had verified, with sunshine in your heart, sometimes the cup even "runneth over"—with *lemonade!*

> You can live a happy life
> In this world of toil and strife,
> If there's sunshine in your heart;
> And your soul will glow with love
> From the perfect Light above,
> If there's sunshine in your heart today.
> (*Hymns*, no. 228)

EPILOGUE

On 14 December 1998, this book was almost finished when the crooked, rocky road of mortality rerouted my life onto a totally unexpected and unwelcome uphill detour. My husband, Elder Dallas N. Archibald of the First Quorum of the Seventy and president of the Chile Area, had been in southern Chile for a weekend of stake conferences and meetings. He stayed over until Monday to enjoy a summer morning of fishing on the beautiful Bio Bio River with President David K. Broadbent of the Chile Concepcion Mission. Shortly after noon on that day, I was notified that, in some unexplainable way, Dallas had been separated from his fishing float tube and, in the process of swimming the short distance to shore, had been swept around a bend in the river and disappeared. A two-hour search had failed to locate him.

Dallas, like Ayrton and Brazil, was sunshine. He could create enthusiasm and joy even in the midst of disaster. He could always turn darkness into day. I can only suppose that I had not learned the sunshine principles directly from him years earlier, solely due to the walls I had erected and my own stubbornness. He was my sunshine, and on December 14, I found it difficult to believe that a beautiful Chilean river could have taken his light and his life. I refused to give up hope, even as hours turned into days. I held onto sunshine, knowing the outcome was in the Lord's hands. While rescue teams thoroughly searched the river and its borders, I cleaned and recleaned our Santiago apartment, went to the temple, and tried to eat and sleep a little.

After spending a couple of Christmas seasons away from family, Dallas and I had planned to enjoy the 1998 holidays in Utah and would have departed Santiago on December 16. I waited until December 18, then, still with no news from the river, I flew north.

On Sunday, December 20, Dallas's body was finally found, floating on the tranquil blue-green surface of the river, in a narrow, golden canyon not too many yards from where he was last seen. He was the first general authority to die in an accident in sixty years. With the search over and the waiting ended, for a moment in time I endured a total eclipse of my sun. Tears flowed as I accepted the truth and mourned my loss. Then, as quickly as I could, I gathered up all the sunshine principles and found that the glittering rays of gratitude truly shattered the darkness. Love. Lemonade. Spontaneity. Sunshine. Joy! I knew I was strong enough to find the silver lining.

The magic sustained me while I waited for the plane carrying his casket to arrive from South America. It sustained me as I spoke at the funeral: "In the perspective of eternity, it won't be very long until we're together again." Our daughter, Teresa Dawn, found her own sunshine, and it sustained her as she said her own personal good-byes and followed my brief remarks with her own: "He had a way of turning life into a wonderful, beautiful thing." We both knew, without doubt, that he had been called to a new and special mission.

Throngs came to bid him farewell—at the funeral in Salt Lake City and at memorial services held in Chile and Brazil. Everywhere there was a sense of disbelief because he had made every day brighter and more beautiful. For many, he was their sunshine. He loved them unconditionally.

My daughter and I chose yellow flowers for the funeral—a little sunshine for a cold December day. A ribbon in the blossoms proclaimed, in Portuguese, her adoration: "Valeu, Papai." ("It was worth it, Daddy.") Other familiar phrases were written in my mind: "Life is eternal. I'll see you soon"; and "I miss you. But there is joy in heaven!"

And one of the first thoughts that came into my mind when I was told he was missing remained, only now transposed: *Is he with Ayrton?* became *He is with Ayrton!* What sunshine they will create together!

Through the days of wondering and waiting, the days of planning and preparing, the days of funeral and farewell, the days of returning to Brazil and Chile to pack my things and dispose of his, and finally the days of leaving South America to begin anew in North America, I learned that I had indeed written the truth months before: "With sunshine in your heart, sometimes the cup even runneth over with lemonade." In my deep personal crisis, the magic worked. I made the pathway bright and maintained my equilibrium through it all. If I could have, I would have drawn a wispy valentine heart in the clear, blue sky as a token of my undying love and appreciation:

"Thanks, Ayrton, Brazil, and especially Dallas,—for the *joy!*"

INDEX

INDEX

INDEX